A Doctor's Guide To Financial Health

DR. DEEPTHI RAO GORUKANTI

ISBN
Hardcase 979-8-89777-904-8
Paperback 979-8-89699-547-0

Contents

PART 01
DIAGNOSIS – UNDERSTANDING THE SYMPTOMS OF FINANCIAL STRESS

Chapter 1: **The Middle-Class Reality:**

Stories of Kavita, Rajiv and Ayesha: Emotional Barometers of Money

- Living Pay Check to Pay Check: Ramesh's Treadmill of Financial Anxiety

- Struggles with Debt: The Consumer Loan Trap-Priya's Story of Endless EMIs

- Emotional Spending vs. Mindful Choices: Suresh and Meena's Tale of Pampering Over Practicality

- Why Financial Literacy is the Missing Piece?

PART 02
BUDGETING, DEBT MANAGEMENT, AND INVESTING IN YOURSELF

- Budgeting illusion in fun vs fundamental buckets
- How to recognise the difference?
- Practical tools for simplified budgeting

- Stories of Good and Bad Debt (e.g. Priya's Dream Home vs. Ramesh's Fancy Car)
- Strategies to pay off debts.

- Turning Hobbies into Hustles
- Physical and mental health: the foundations of sustained financial growth
- Time management: balancing wealth and well-being
- Establishing Safety Nets for Life: emergency funds, health insurance, term insurance
- Tax optimisation in India

PART 03
WEALTH CREATION – INVESTMENTS, FIRE, AND PORTFOLIO MANAGEMENT

PART 04
FINANCIAL FITNESS FOR LIFE

About the Author

Dr. Deepthi Rao Gorukanti is a dynamic professional whose journey bridges the worlds of medicine, business, and global affairs. A specialist in Internal Medicine (MD) with a deep passion for patient care, she has expanded her expertise to encompass the realms of finance, leadership, and diplomacy.

With an MBA that honed her strategic and management skills, and a Diploma in International Affairs and Diplomacy, Dr. Deepthi brings a truly global perspective to her work. She is not only a professor but also an entrepreneur, dedicated to empowering others through education, innovation, and practical solutions.

A natural communicator, Dr. Deepthi is also a blogger, sharing insights on life's big questions, from happiness and purpose to relationships and personal growth. Her writing combines wisdom, empathy, and humour, making complex ideas easy to understand and apply.

Through her book, *A Doctor's Guide to Financial Health*, she draws on her unique blend of experiences to simplify finance for beginners. Whether it's teaching, mentoring, or writing, Dr. Deepthi's mission is clear: to help people thrive, one step at a time.

When she's not busy inspiring others, you'll find her exploring new ideas, savouring a quiet sunrise, or dreaming of her next big adventure.

Introduction

Money: The Ticket to Dreams, Freedom, and a Lot of Stress

Let's be honest; money is *complicated*. It's not just numbers in your bank account; it's what those numbers mean. A better life for your family, a big fat *yes* to your dream home, or that once-in-a-lifetime Europe trip you've been secretly planning in your head. Money isn't everything, sure, but it's hard to argue when it can pay for your kid's education abroad or buy you the freedom to quit a job you hate.

The Dreams Money Can Achieve

Picture this: your son or daughter, studying at a top university in the U.S., is walking across that graduation stage, and you are sitting in the audience, cheering with pride. That's not just a dream—it's a dream *money* can make real. Or think about that villa you've always wanted, with a garden where you sip chai in the mornings or host weekend barbecues. Or even something simpler but just as meaningful—a long-overdue vacation with your parents to Kerala, Goa, or maybe even Paris.

These dreams aren't about being "rich." They're about wanting a good life for yourself and your loved ones. And let's face it, these dreams come with price tags.

What Does "Enough Money" Really Mean?

For most of us, "enough" isn't about driving a Lamborghini or owning 10 mansions. It's about not worrying constantly. It's about being able to send your kids to a good school, have some savings for emergencies, or take a break and travel when life feels too heavy. It's about breathing easily at the end of the month, knowing you're not drowning in EMIs or bills.

When you have enough money, it gives you freedom—the kind that lets you make decisions without fear. Want to quit that toxic job? Done. Want to help your parents with medical expenses? No stress. Want to invest in your passion for cooking and finally open that little café? Go for it.

Why Managing Money Feels Like Climbing Everest

But here's the catch: managing money is not easy. It's one thing to earn it and another to make it last. You might start with a budget, but then life happens. A wedding to attend here, a medical emergency there, and before you know it, you're wondering where all your savings disappeared.

Add to that the temptation of online shopping sales, EMI schemes that make you think you're saving when you're really spending more, and Instagram influencers showing off their luxury vacations—it's no surprise that managing money feels overwhelming.

Mishandling Money: A Recipe for Stress

And let's be real: when money is mishandled, it can turn into a nightmare. Picture this: overspending on a credit card to buy that flashy new phone and then struggling to pay it off while interest piles up. Or saying yes to every loan offer without thinking about how you'll repay it. Mismanaging money doesn't just mess up your finances—it can strain relationships, ruin opportunities, and leave you feeling stuck in a cycle of stress and regret.

A Personal Note:

Money isn't just about numbers; it's about emotions. The pride of buying your first home. The joy of treating your family to a special vacation. The peace of knowing you've secured a good education for your kids. It's not about being the richest person in the room – it's about using money to live the life you want with the people you love.

So, whether you're saving up for a car, planning a trip, or just trying to get through the month without dipping into your savings, remember: it's not about how much money you have, but how well you use it. A little planning, a little discipline, and a lot of self-belief can go a long way.

But where do we start, how do we go ahead, what are rational choices, what are reasonable trade-offs in that path? Most of us struggle because our schools and colleges never equipped us with the most important skill: how to manage money. Our parents stressed on studying hard and getting a good job. Our mentors taught us how to perform in an interview and how to negotiate a good salary. But no one taught us how to manage money, which is as important as oxygen for our lives. Who do we even ask for advice? Social media influencers who can sell any scam to us? Or neighbours or colleagues or relatives because it's easy to stay in the herd even though most of them don't know what's driving their money decisions? Books or websites which made finance into the highest form of jargon which a layman can never understand?

Trust me, I have been there. I suffered from bad choices, bad advice, and made it a mission to understand the complex human body, its systems, diseases, complications, and cures. If I can comprehend medicine, why not finance? How can it be tougher than medicine? That made me pursue an MBA, take numerous courses, read many books, and over the years, gain knowledge and skills to optimise it for my own life. This book is my attempt to share that knowledge with you in the most simplified, understandable, and relatable language because I understand the pain involved in understanding the complicated world of finance, where money is intentionally mystified, and only the glorified rich have all access while we commoners are deprived. I believe knowledge is for all, and it should be available, affordable, and understandable for everyone to make informed choices in their lives.

This is not an easy path to riches; it's a guiding light to your journey towards your dreams.

Why Financial Health is as Crucial as Physical Health?

We visit doctors to care for our bodies, ensuring we eat right, exercise, and stay healthy. But how often do we consider the health of our finances? Just as high blood pressure or diabetes silently harms physical health, poor financial health creeps into our lives, creating stress and limiting choices. Let's face it—no amount of yoga can ease the anxiety of a mounting credit card bill or an empty savings account during an emergency.

Financial health isn't just about how much you earn; it's about how you manage, save, and grow your wealth. It's the foundation of a life where you can chase dreams, support loved ones, and face challenges with confidence. Think of it as the heartbeat of your lifestyle. Just as your physical heart pumps blood to keep you alive, financial health powers your aspirations, giving you the freedom to live with purpose and peace of mind.

Why Financial Health is Gaining Global Importance?

In today's world, financial health is more critical than ever. Rising medical costs, economic uncertainty, and inflation are creating unprecedented challenges for individuals and families alike. Unexpected health crises can drain savings in an instant, leaving people vulnerable to debt and financial stress. Meanwhile, global economic shifts, from market volatility to job insecurities, are compelling everyone to rethink how they save, invest, and spend.

Moreover, the pandemic has underscored the importance of emergency funds, insurance, and diversified investments. As the cost of living rises and traditional retirement safety nets weaken, achieving financial health is no longer a luxury but a necessity for a secure and fulfilling life.

A Doctor's Journey into Personal Finance

Let me make a confession: Doctors are often seen as poor financial planners, and I was no exception. Like many others, I assumed that earning a stable income would naturally lead to financial security. I was wrong.

Coming from a middle-class background, I saw my parents save every penny to provide us with a roof over our heads and a good education. When I started earning, I thought I had "made it." I splurged on luxury gadgets, vacations, and even a car, believing I deserved the best after years of hard work. Life was good—until it wasn't. When an unexpected financial storm hit, I found myself borrowing from my parents despite earning a handsome salary. That humbling experience made me realise that financial success isn't about how much you earn but how wisely you manage what you have.

Over time, I learned to balance my personal and professional aspirations, discovering that financial health is deeply intertwined with overall well-being. As a doctor, I've always cared for my patients' mental and physical health. Now, I understand that financial stability plays an equally vital role in a person's happiness and peace of mind.

The Purpose of This Book

This book is my honest attempt to help you avoid the financial pitfalls I faced. It's not about turning you into a billionaire or a stock market wizard. Instead, it's about guiding you toward a balanced, fulfilling life – a life where you achieve your goals, maintain your health, and spend quality time with loved ones, all while ensuring your finances are secure.

Think of this book as your companion for building wealth for well-being. It's designed to simplify complex financial concepts and provide actionable advice tailored to the Indian middle class. You'll learn to:

- Diagnose the symptoms of financial stress and treat them effectively.

- Create a budget that balances enjoyment and responsibility.

- Build an investment portfolio suited to your goals and risk tolerance.

- Understand the power of compounding and early financial planning.

- Safeguard your future with the right insurance and emergency funds.

Together, we'll embark on a journey to achieve financial health – a journey where every rupee saved today is a step towards a brighter, more secure tomorrow. And just like in medicine, the smallest lifestyle changes can lead to profound transformations over time.

Are you ready to take the first step towards financial wellness? Let's begin.

PART 01

DIAGNOSIS – UNDERSTANDING THE SYMPTOMS OF FINANCIAL STRESS

Chapter 1

The Middle-Class Reality: Financial Health in Crisis

For most middle-class Indians, financial health often feels like a mirage – close enough to touch but just out of reach. The struggle is real, and the symptoms of financial stress are everywhere. Let's decode these signs and understand where the real pain points lie.

Money means different things to different people.

- To Kavita, a shopaholic homemaker, it's the thrill of owning the latest kitchen gadget that her neighbours don't have.

- To Rajiv, a government clerk, it's the security of knowing his children can study abroad one day.

- To Ayesha, an ambitious start-up founder, it's the power to scale her dreams.

These varied perceptions drive our choices—sometimes into sound decisions and sometimes into financial quicksand. For the middle class, money isn't just currency; it's an emotional barometer of status, dreams, and fears.

Living Pay Check to Pay Check

Meet Ramesh, a software engineer from Hyderabad. Every month, his salary arrives like clockwork. But by the 25th, he's anxiously counting the days until the next payday. One day, his refrigerator broke down. The repair cost was modest, but for

Ramesh, it meant borrowing money from a friend. This endless cycle of earning and spending left him feeling stuck, like running on a treadmill that never stops. He dreams of saving up for a car, but the reality of rent, bills, and daily expenses keeps crushing that hope.

Struggles with Debt: The Consumer Loan Trap

Take the story of Priya, a working mother from Chennai. When Priya's family bought a new TV, fridge, and air conditioner within six months, she justified it as an investment in comfort and keeping up with her peers. All of it was on EMIs. Soon after, her daughter's school fee demand came in, but Priya had no savings left. She resorted to a personal loan to cover it. By now, her monthly bills were staring at her like unpaid landlords: utility payments, EMIs, groceries, and even a credit card balance that refused to shrink. Each day felt heavier as she grappled with the guilt of poor choices and the anxiety of endless debt.

Emotional Spending vs. Mindful Choices

We've all been there. Take Suresh and Meena, a middle-class couple from Pune. They believed their kids deserved the best, unlike what they had growing up. For their son's birthday, Suresh bought the latest iPhone, and Meena got a designer suit for their daughter's graduation. "They're kids; they need to be pampered," they told themselves. Not stopping there, they arranged a pilgrimage for their elderly parents. While their intentions were noble, the financial aftermath wasn't. When Meena suddenly needed urgent medical attention, they had no savings left to cover the hospital bills. Emotional spending had robbed them of their financial safety net.

Why Financial Literacy is the Missing Piece

Financial stress often thrives on ignorance. Vikram, a taxi driver in Mumbai, worked long hours but had no idea how to save or invest. When the pandemic hit, his income dried up overnight. If only he had a small emergency fund or some savings, his story might have been different. Lack of financial literacy isn't just a problem; it's a crisis.

Vikram's situation worsened when he contracted COVID-19 during the second wave. Without health insurance, he couldn't afford private care and was forced to rely on overcrowded government hospitals. Sadly, Vikram didn't make it. His family was left shattered, not just emotionally but financially. There was no term insurance to help them survive, and they had to sell whatever little assets they owned to cover expenses. Health and term insurance are often overlooked but are vital safeguards against unforeseen crises. Financial literacy includes understanding these tools, ensuring that no family faces such dire circumstances due to a lack of planning.

* * * * *

Chapter 2

Financial Health Checklist

Are you in poor financial health? Here's a quick checklist to self-assess:

1. **Living Pay Check to Pay Check:** Do you struggle to make it to the end of the month without borrowing or cutting corners?

2. **Lack of Emergency Fund:** Do you have at least 3-6 months of living expenses saved up for emergencies?

3. **High Debt-to-Income Ratio:** Is more than 40% of your income going toward EMIs and loans?

4. **No Health or Term Insurance:** Would your family be financially secure if something unexpected happened to you?

5. **Untracked Expenses:** Do you find it difficult to account for where your money goes each month?

6. **Impulse Spending:** Do you often buy things out of emotion rather than necessity, leaving you with buyer's remorse?

7. **No Passive Income:** Are you entirely dependent on active income with no other sources of earnings?

8. **Negative Net Worth:** Are your liabilities greater than your assets?

If you find yourself saying "yes" to any of these questions, it's time to take a hard look at your financial health and start making changes.

* * * *

Chapter 3

The Anatomy of Personal Finance

Like a good health check-up, understanding personal finance requires looking at the whole picture: income, expenses, debt, and net worth. Let's break it down.

Understanding Your Income: Active vs Passive Income

Active income is the money you earn by trading your time and effort, like a salary, consulting fees, or hourly wages. For instance, Arun, a software developer, works nine hours daily and earns a steady salary. While it keeps the lights on, his income entirely depends on his job—no work, no money.

On the other hand, passive income is money earned with minimal effort after an initial investment of time or money. Consider Neha, a marketing executive who started a YouTube channel discussing fitness tips. Initially, she spent weekends creating videos, but now her channel generates regular ad revenue, providing a consistent income stream alongside her job. Combining active and passive income gives financial stability, ensuring you aren't entirely reliant on one source.

Decoding Expenses: Where Your Money Really Goes

Expenses are like leaks in a bucket—a few unnoticed drips, and soon, the bucket is empty. Take Manish, a project manager, who was shocked after reviewing his monthly expenses. While he thought groceries and bills were his biggest costs, it turned out his daily coffee runs, food delivery apps, and unused gym memberships were eating away at his salary.

By switching to home-brewed coffee and cancelling unnecessary subscriptions, he saved enough for a vacation in just six months. Tracking expenses allows you to find and fix these "leaks," giving you more control over your finances.

The Debt-to-Income Imbalance: How Much Debt is Too Much?

A high Debt-to-Income (DTI) ratio can choke your financial freedom. Anjali, a boutique owner, experienced this firsthand. She took out multiple loans—one to start her boutique and others for personal expenses. Soon, her EMIs consumed 60% of her monthly income, leaving her with little to reinvest in her business or save.

With expert guidance, she consolidated her loans and reduced her DTI ratio to 30%. This freed up cash for savings and investments, allowing her to expand her business. Aim for a DTI ratio below 40% to avoid becoming a slave to debt.

Net Worth: Your Financial "Vital Signs"

Think of net worth as the heartbeat of your financial health. For instance, Rohit, a retired banker, has a positive net worth due to years of disciplined investing. This allows him to comfortably support his grandchildren's education.

In contrast, Shruti, a young professional, realised her net worth was negative after accounting for her student loans and credit card debt. Understanding this helped her prioritise paying off debt and start building assets like savings and mutual funds. Regularly calculating net worth can motivate you to reduce liabilities and grow your assets.

Understanding these fundamentals is the first step towards taking control of your financial health. Just like diagnosing a patient, identifying these symptoms helps you focus on the right treatment plan. Remember, awareness is the beginning of all change. You are not alone in this journey—and every small step counts.

* * * * *

PART 02

BUDGETING, DEBT MANAGEMENT, AND INVESTING IN YOURSELF

Chapter 4

Budgeting: The Fundamental, Fun, and Future Buckets

Budgeting sounds like a boring lecture on numbers, but trust me, it's more like planning a party for your money. Imagine your finances as guests, each invited to three main rooms: **Fundamental**, **Fun**, and **Future**. Let's explore these buckets and how to manage them with real-life examples and practical tools.

1. Fundamental Bucket: Needs First, Always

This is the survival kit of your budget. Think of your needs—those non-negotiables that keep life running smoothly.

What goes in this bucket?

- Rent or home loan EMI

- Utilities like electricity, water, and internet

- Groceries

- Health insurance premiums

- Basic transportation (fuel or metro card)

Real-Life Example:

Ravi, a middle-class IT professional, earns ₹50,000 per month. His Fundamental Bucket includes:

- ₹12,000 for rent
- ₹3,000 for utilities
- ₹5,000 for groceries
- ₹2,000 for commuting
- ₹3,000 for health insurance

This totals ₹25,000—50% of his income. He ensures these expenses don't exceed half his pay check, leaving room for the other buckets.

2. Fun Bucket: Because Life Needs Joy

This bucket funds your wants, not your needs. Think of it as the spice in your budgeting recipe. It includes everything that makes life enjoyable: eating out, Netflix subscriptions, hobbies, or that gorgeous kurta you've been eyeing.

What goes in this bucket?

- Dining out or food delivery
- Entertainment (movies, subscriptions)
- Shopping (clothes, gadgets, home décor)
- Hobbies (painting, yoga classes)

Real-Life Example:

Neha, a school teacher earning ₹40,000, dedicates ₹8,000 (20% of her income) to her Fun Bucket:

- ₹2,000 for Netflix and Spotify
- ₹3,000 for dining out twice a month
- ₹1,500 for her weekend pottery class
- ₹1,500 for impulsive shopping

By budgeting for fun, Neha doesn't feel guilty when she splurges occasionally.

3. Future Bucket: A Better Tomorrow

This bucket prepares you for long-term goals and emergencies. Whether it's saving for retirement, a child's education, or that dream solo trip to Bali, this bucket is your financial safety net.

What goes in this bucket?

- Emergency fund
- Retirement investments (PPF, NPS, mutual funds)
- Savings for big goals (buying a car, funding education)
- Debt repayment (if applicable)

Real-Life Example:

Rajesh and Maya, a middle-class couple earning ₹80,000 combined, allocate ₹24,000 (30% of their income) to their Future Bucket:

- ₹6,000 to a recurring deposit for their emergency fund
- ₹10,000 to mutual funds for retirement
- ₹4,000 towards their child's education
- ₹4,000 as an additional EMI on their home loan to reduce debt faster

This disciplined allocation ensures they have peace of mind, no matter what life throws at them.

How We Confuse Fun with Fundamental: The Budgeting Illusion

When it comes to money, our emotions often play tricks on us. We convince ourselves that certain **wants** are actually **needs**, and before we know it, our Fun Bucket is masquerading as our Fundamental Bucket. Let's break this down with some common situations and see how we often justify spending on non-essentials as essentials.

1. Clothes: The "I Need It for Work" Excuse

- **How We Confuse:** Buying new clothes for every festival, office event, or wedding and labelling them as "necessary."

- **Reality:** You probably have ten kurtas, five sarees, or enough shirts already in your wardrobe to look stunning. Adding one more isn't survival—it's indulgence.

Real-Life Example:

Radhika, a teacher, convinced herself she needed a ₹3,000 saree for her school's annual day because "it's part of the culture." In truth, she could have worn something she already had. That ₹3,000 was a Fun Bucket expense, not fundamental.

2. Salons: "Looking Presentable is Important"

- **How We Confuse:** Regular facials, hair spa treatments, or fancy manicures feel like they're essential to maintaining hygiene.

- **Reality:** A basic haircut or DIY skincare routine can keep you groomed without blowing ₹5,000 a month.

Real-Life Example:

Aparna feels her ₹1,500 monthly manicure is necessary because "well-maintained nails show professionalism." However, a simple ₹100 nail cutter and polish can achieve the same result.

3. Festival Expenses: "It's a Tradition"

- **How We Confuse:** Buying expensive decorations, gifting lavishly, or hosting grand feasts in the name of tradition.

- **Reality:** Celebrations can be meaningful without breaking the bank. Handmade decorations or small get-togethers with family can keep the spirit alive.

Real-Life Example:

During Diwali, Arjun spent ₹15,000 on lighting, gifting, and sweets, believing it was necessary to "uphold tradition." But a few LED diyas and homemade sweets could have done the trick for ₹3,000.

4. Birthdays and Anniversaries: "It's a Special Day"

- **How We Confuse:** Splurging on elaborate parties, expensive cakes, or gifts because "we deserve to celebrate."

- **Reality:** Celebrating doesn't have to mean spending excessively. A cosy dinner at home or a heartfelt handwritten card can make the day equally memorable.

Real-Life Example:

Ravi threw a ₹20,000 party for his wife's birthday, justifying it as an essential expense because "she deserves it." A small gathering with close friends or a romantic evening for ₹5,000 would have been just as meaningful.

5. Kids' Demands: "They Need It for School"

- **How We Confuse:** Buying kids the latest gadgets, branded clothes, or fancy school supplies because "they need to keep up."

- **Reality:** Kids don't need a ₹2,000 school bag or a ₹15,000 tablet unless it's genuinely required for education.

Real-Life Example:

Suresh bought his son an iPad, claiming it was for online classes. The iPad quickly became a gaming device, proving the expense was more about indulgence than necessity.

6. Gifting: "It's Obligatory"

- **How We Confuse:** Feeling pressured to buy expensive gifts for weddings, housewarmings, or birthdays because "it's expected."
- **Reality:** Thoughtful, budget-friendly gifts are just as appreciated.

Real-Life Example:

Priya spent ₹5,000 on a wedding gift for a colleague she barely knew, rationalising it as "maintaining social connections." A personalised ₹1,000 gift would have been sufficient.

7. Eating Out: "It's Convenient"

- **How We Confuse:** Dining out or ordering in under the pretence of being "too busy to cook."
- **Reality:** Preparing simple meals at home is healthier and far cheaper.

Real-Life Example:

Vikram spent ₹10,000 monthly on Zomato orders, claiming he had no time to cook. By meal prepping on weekends, he cut this expense to ₹2,500.

8. Technology Upgrades: "I Need the Latest Version"

- **How We Confuse:** Upgrading smartphones, laptops, or gadgets because "it's faster" or "the camera is better."
- **Reality:** Your existing device likely works fine. Upgrades are rarely urgent.

Real-Life Example:

Rohan upgraded his perfectly functional phone to the latest iPhone, thinking it was essential for work. In truth, his old phone handled emails and calls just as well.

9. Home Décor: "We Need to Keep the House Presentable"

- **How We Confuse:** Spending on expensive showpieces, curtains, or furniture updates because "guests are coming."
- **Reality:** A clean and tidy home is more impressive than pricey décor.

Real-Life Example:

Meena spent ₹8,000 on new cushions and curtains before hosting a party, calling it a necessity. Her old cushions were perfectly usable.

10. Travel: "I Need a Break"

- **How We Confuse:** Booking luxurious trips or frequent getaways as a "mental health necessity."
- **Reality:** Budget-friendly trips or local day trips can also rejuvenate you.

Real-Life Example:

Shweta splurged ₹50,000 on a Goa trip, convincing herself she needed it to de-stress. A weekend trek for ₹5,000 would have served the same purpose.

How to Recognise the Difference?

1. **Ask Yourself: Can I Live Without It?**

    o   If the answer is yes, it's likely a Fun Bucket expense.

2. **Delay the Decision:**

    o   Wait 24-48 hours before making a purchase. You may realise it's not as essential as you thought.

3. **Use the "Substitute Test":**

    o   Can you achieve the same purpose with a cheaper alternative? If yes, it's not fundamental.

Conclusion: Fun Masquerading as Fundamental

The middle class often struggles with financial discipline because of the blurred line between needs and wants. By recognising and categorising expenses correctly, you can take control of your finances. The key is to stop emotional justifications and focus on real priorities.

A good rule of thumb: **Spend on what you need, save for what you want, and invest for what you dream.**

Practical Tools for Simplified Budgeting

1. Budgeting Apps

–   Good budget: Perfect for envelope budgeting—allocates money to categories (buckets) virtually.

–   Money Manager: Tracks expenses in real time.

–   Walnut: Links to your bank and credit card to analyse spending habits.

2. Spreadsheets

A simple Excel or Google Sheets template works wonders. Create columns for income, categories, and actual expenses. Use formulas to track spending and highlight areas where you overspend.

Category	Bucket	Planned Amount (₹)	Actual Amount (₹)
Rent	Fundamental	12000	12000
Utilities	Fundamental	3000	3200
Groceries	Fundamental	5000	4500
Insurance	Fundamental	2000	2000
Dining Out	Fun	3000	3500
Subscriptions	Fun	1000	1500
Shopping	Fun	2000	2500
Emergency Fund	Future	5000	4000
Investments	Future	8000	8500
Retirement Savings	Future	5000	5500

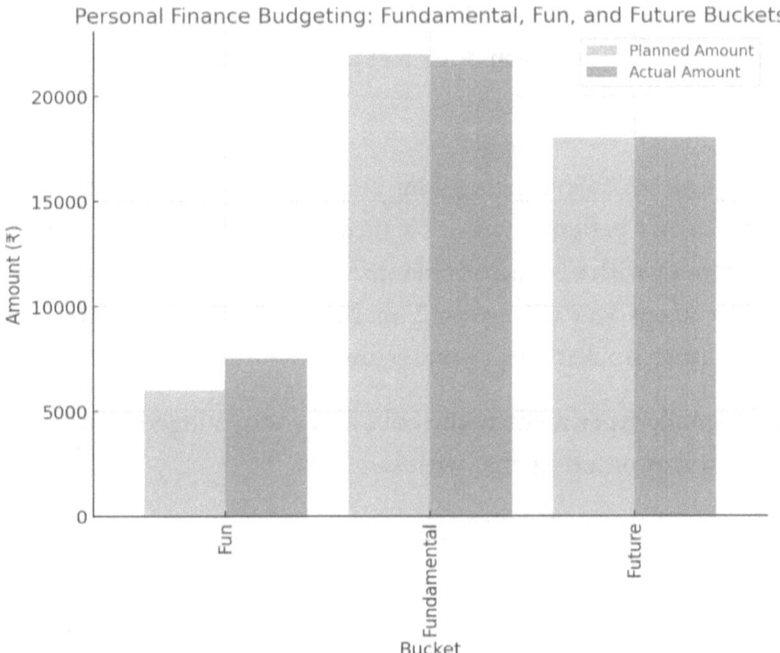

3. Budget Challenges

Gamify your budgeting to make it fun:

- No-Spend Week Challenge: Spend only on essentials for a week.

- 52-Week Savings Challenge: Save a specific amount (e.g., ₹500) each week and increase it gradually.

- Cash-Only Challenge: Withdraw cash for expenses and stick to it.

Why Budgeting Works

Budgeting is like giving your money a GPS—every rupee knows where to go. It avoids overspending, reduces debt, and creates opportunities for financial growth. Plus, it balances enjoyment and responsibility, so you don't feel deprived or stressed.

Final Thoughts

Budgeting isn't about being stingy; it's about being smart. Like a doctor treats patients with a balance of medicine and care, treat your money with a balance of planning and fun. Your Fundamental Bucket keeps you alive, your Fun Bucket keeps you happy, and your Future Bucket keeps you secure.

Start small, experiment with tools, and soon, budgeting will feel as natural as ordering chai with samosas.

* * * * *

Chapter 5

The Debt Detox: Breaking Free from Consumer Loans

Debt is like fire. When controlled, it can cook food, light your home, and keep you warm. But left unchecked, it can burn everything to the ground. Let's explore how good debt can help build a future and how bad debt can derail it—through personal stories.

Good Debt: Stories That Inspire

1. Priya's Dream Home:

Priya, a teacher, always dreamed of owning a house. When she found the perfect 2BHK in Hyderabad, she hesitated to take a ₹30 lakh home loan. But, after crunching numbers, she realised the monthly EMI was manageable within her budget.

Fast forward 10 years: the value of her home doubled, and she now has an asset to her name. The loan felt heavy at first, but it gave her a roof, a sense of security, and an appreciating investment.

Lesson: A home loan can be a smart move if you buy within your means.

2. Arjun's Higher Studies:

Arjun, an engineer from a small town, got admitted to a prestigious MBA programme. The ₹15 lakh education loan felt like a mountain, but he saw it as a ticket to a better life.

After graduation, Arjun landed a job with a salary of ₹20 lakh per year. He paid off the loan in four years and now earns three times what he would have without the degree.

Lesson: Education loans can unlock opportunities, but choose wisely—don't borrow for a degree with no clear Return on Investment (ROI).

Bad Debt: Stories That Warn

1. Meena's Shopping Spree:

Meena loved to keep up with trends. Every month, she maxed out her credit card, buying branded clothes, gadgets, and fancy dinners. She thought, *"It's just ₹5,000 more. I'll pay it off next month."*

Within a year, her credit card debt snowballed to ₹2 lakh, with 36% interest. To clear it, she had to take a personal loan, which added more stress to her monthly budget.

Lesson: Bad debt often starts small. If it doesn't grow your wealth or improve your life significantly, it's not worth it.

2. Ramesh's Fancy Car:

Ramesh, a young professional, wanted to impress his friends. He took a ₹10 lakh loan for a luxury car, even though his salary was ₹40,000 per month. The monthly EMI took up almost half of his income, leaving little for savings or emergencies. When his company downsized, Ramesh had to sell the car at a loss, leaving him with no car and leftover debt.

Lesson: A car is a depreciating asset. Borrowing for a basic necessity is fine, but stretching for luxury can backfire.

Blended Story: The Debt Journey of Dr. Nisha

Dr. Nisha, a dentist, had a mix of good and bad debts. She took a ₹10 lakh education loan to study dentistry, which she repaid in five years thanks to her clinic's steady income.

However, she also fell into the trap of using a personal loan for a lavish clinic renovation. Instead of sticking to her budget, she overspent on premium furniture and décor to compete with fancier clinics in her area. The renovation loan cost her ₹3 lakh in unnecessary interest over three years.

Looking back, she says, *"My education loan gave me wings, but the personal loan tied me down. Now, I invest wisely in my clinic without over-borrowing."*

Lesson: Good debt builds your future; bad debt complicates it.

Final Thought:

Good debt is like a pair of running shoes – it helps you move forward. Bad debt is like a pair of tight, flashy shoes – they look good but give you blisters. By learning from these stories, you can identify which debts to embrace and which to avoid.

So, what's your story going to be? Will you run towards financial freedom or stumble over flashy distractions? Choose wisely!

Strategies to Pay Off Debt

Paying off debt is like climbing a mountain – it takes effort, strategy, and a lot of determination. Here are detailed approaches to help you knock out debt, with examples to keep it relatable.

1. Snowball Method: Small Wins for Big Motivation

The **snowball method** focuses on paying off your smallest debts first, regardless of their interest rates. Why? Because clearing a debt entirely gives you a psychological boost that keeps you motivated to tackle the rest.

Steps to Apply the Snowball Method:

1. List all your debts from smallest to largest, ignoring interest rates.

2. Pay the minimum on all debts except the smallest one.

3. Channel any extra money into paying off the smallest debt.

4. Once the smallest debt is cleared, roll that amount into the next smallest debt.

   Example:

   - Credit Card A: ₹5,000 at 15% interest.
   - Credit Card B: ₹10,000 at 20% interest.
   - Personal Loan: ₹50,000 at 12% interest.

   Action Plan:

   - Focus on Credit Card A first. Let's say you pay ₹2,500/month. In two months, it's gone!
   - Then move to Credit Card B, using the ₹2,500 you freed up, plus the regular payment for Credit Card B.
   - Finally, tackle the personal loan with the full amount.

   Why It Works:

   - The quick wins keep you energised. Debt feels manageable because you see progress early.

2. Avalanche Method: Save on Interest

The **avalanche method** targets debts with the highest interest rates first, saving you the most money in the long run.

Steps to Apply the Avalanche Method:

1. List your debts from the highest interest rate to the lowest.
2. Pay the minimum on all debts except the one with the highest interest rate.
3. Direct all extra money to the high-interest debt.
4. Once the highest-interest debt is paid, move to the next one.

Example:

- Credit Card A: ₹5,000 at 20% interest.
- Credit Card B: ₹10,000 at 15% interest.
- Personal Loan: ₹50,000 at 12% interest.

Action Plan:

- Attack Credit Card A first. Put every extra rupee toward this debt while making minimum payments on the others.
- After clearing it, use the freed-up amount to pay off Credit Card B.
- Finally, tackle the personal loan.

Why It Works:

- You minimise interest payments, saving money in the long run.

3. The Hybrid Approach

Can't decide between snowball and avalanche? Mix them! Start with the snowball method to build momentum, then switch to the avalanche method for maximum savings.

Action plan:

- First, clear a small, nagging debt (like ₹3,000 credit card dues).
- Once you've tasted success, switch gears and prioritise the debt with the highest interest rate.

Why It Works:

- You get the best of both worlds: early motivation and long-term savings.

4. Debt Consolidation

If you have multiple debts with high interest rates, consider consolidating them into one loan with a lower interest rate. This simplifies payments and can save money on interest.

Action plan:

Ravi had three credit cards with an average interest rate of 24%. He took a personal loan at 12% interest and used it to pay off all his credit cards.

Why It Works?

Now, he focuses on one manageable loan instead of juggling multiple payments.

Caution:

- Avoid running up new debt after consolidating, or you'll end up with double trouble.

5. Balance Transfer

For credit card debt, a **balance transfer** can help. Many banks offer promotional periods with 0% or low interest on balance transfers.

Action plan:

Meera had ₹1,00,000 in credit card debt at 18% interest. She transferred it to a new credit card offering 6 months at 0% interest. She paid ₹20,000 per month during this period and cleared the debt without paying any extra interest.

Why It Works?

You can repay debt without extra interest.

Caution:

- Be sure you can pay off the debt during the promotional period, or the interest will spike.

6. Side Hustle Your Way Out

If your income isn't enough to clear your debts, consider a side hustle. From freelancing to tutoring or selling handmade crafts, every extra rupee helps.

Action plan:

- Rohit, a marketing professional, took up freelance graphic designing over weekends. The ₹10,000 he earned monthly went directly towards his ₹1,50,000 personal loan, cutting his repayment time in half.

Why It Works?

A side hustle can be fewer work hours, significant income other than salary to help you clear debts.

7. Automate Payments

Automating payments ensures you don't miss due dates, avoiding late fees and penalties. Set up standing instructions for EMIs and minimum payments, so your debt is always under control.

Action plan:

Anita automated her ₹8,000 EMI for a personal loan. She adjusted her monthly expenses accordingly and never faced the stress of forgotten payments.

Why It Works?

Automation avoids late fee charges and the stress of remembering all payment dates.

8. Negotiate for Better Terms

Don't hesitate to call your lender to negotiate lower interest rates or a more flexible repayment plan.

Action plan:

Ajay's personal loan was at 14% interest. After two years of on-time payments, he requested a rate reduction. The bank reduced it to 12%, saving him thousands over the loan tenure.

Why It Works?

Interest lowering can save a significant amount of money when it's a long-term loan over many years.

9. Sell What You Don't Need

Declutter your life and sell unused items to make extra cash.

Action plan:

Simran sold her old smartphone, laptop, and unused gym equipment online, earning ₹25,000. She used the money to pay off part of her credit card debt.

Why It Works?

Decluttering your space of unused items gives you some extra bucks and frees your space and mind.

10. Create a "No-Spend" Month

Commit to a no-spend challenge where you avoid all non-essential expenses for one month. Use the saved money to pay off debt.

Action plan:

During her no-spend month, Kavitha cut out dining out, entertainment subscriptions, and shopping. She saved ₹15,000 and used it to clear a chunk of her ₹50,000 credit card bill.

Why It Works?

We need to set our own rules to avoid impulse spending and peer pressure. It's easy to tell your peers that you have taken up a no-spend challenge rather than saying you have debts.

Key Takeaway

Every rupee you pay off is a step closer to freedom. Pick a strategy that matches your personality—snowball for motivation, avalanche for savings, or a mix of both. Add creativity to your journey with side hustles, negotiations, and challenges. Remember, paying off debt isn't just about numbers; it's about building a financially free and stress-free life.

What's your first step going to be? Start now!

Building a Debt-Free Mindset: Turn "Oh No!" into "Oh Yes!"

Becoming debt-free isn't just about crunching numbers; it's about reprogramming your brain. Think of it as upgrading your mental software from *Debt 1.0* (impulse buys and EMIs) to *Wealth 2.0* (freedom and savings). Let's dive in with a mix of humour and wisdom!

1. Stop Competing with the Neighbours

They got a new car? Great, let them enjoy it (and their EMIs). You don't need to keep up unless they're paying your loans too!

Insight:

"Keeping up with the Sharmas" is an expensive reality show where you're the only contestant—and the loser if you're borrowing to compete.

Mindset Shift:

Focus on your goals, not others' Instagram-worthy lives. A debt-free selfie is the real flex.

2. Treat Credit Cards Like a Hot Sauce Bottle

Credit cards are like hot sauce: a little bit is fine, but too much, and you're in serious trouble. Swipe wisely and sparingly.

Insight:

Ever noticed how a ₹500 bill turns into ₹5,000 when you pay the minimum due? That's the interest laughing behind your back.

Mindset Shift:

Use credit only when you can pay it off in full. If you can't afford it today, you probably can't afford it tomorrow, either.

3. Develop the "Do I Need It?" Reflex

Before buying anything, ask yourself, *"Do I need it, or do I just want it?"* If the answer is "want," walk away.

Insight:

Your wardrobe doesn't need a 17th pair of black shoes. Your financial future, however, does need that ₹5,000.

Mindset Shift:

Pause before purchases. The thrill of saving lasts longer than the thrill of buying.

4. Budget Like a Chef

A good chef uses ingredients wisely—nothing wasted, everything purposeful. Treat your money the same way.

Insight:

Think of your income as biryani rice. If you overspend on spices (wants), you won't have enough for the meat (needs).

Mindset Shift:

Budgeting isn't boring – it's the recipe for financial success. Make it a game to see how much you can save each month.

5. Build an Emergency Fund

Life throws curveballs – medical bills, car repairs, or your friend's wedding in Goa. Be ready for them.

Insight:

Without an emergency fund, every small crisis feels like an earthquake. With one, it's just a hiccup.

Mindset Shift:

Start with ₹500 or ₹1,000 a month. Watching it grow feels like raising a baby – less messy and equally rewarding.

6. Celebrate the Small Wins

Paid off a credit card? Cleared a loan? Celebrate! But keep it simple—no "debt-free" trips to the Maldives yet.

Insight:

Reward yourself with a ₹200 treat, not a ₹20,000 expense. Otherwise, you're just running on a debt treadmill.

Mindset Shift:

Progress is progress, no matter how small. Celebrate with a happy dance, not a shopping spree.

7. Learn to Say "No"

Your friend wants to split a fancy dinner bill, and your cousin wants you to sponsor their latest scheme? Politely decline.

Insight:

Saying "no" to others is easier than saying "no" to collection agents later.

Mindset Shift:

Your financial health matters more than someone else's temporary happiness. Say "no" with a smile and a firm hand.

8. Visualise the Freedom

Imagine a life where you're not worried about due dates, minimum payments, or high interest. Feels good, right?

Insight:

Debt freedom is like quitting junk food – it's tough at first, but eventually, you feel lighter, healthier, and happier.

Mindset Shift:

Create a vision board with your goals: a debt-free life, a vacation, or even just peace of mind. Look at it whenever you're tempted to spend.

9. Surround Yourself with Like-Minded People

If your friends think "YOLO" means splurge today, debt tomorrow, it's time to find new company.

Insight:

Financially responsible friends won't drag you to fancy restaurants – they'll drag you to a budget-friendly chai *tapri*.

Mindset Shift:

Build a circle of people who inspire you to save, invest, and grow. Their habits will rub off on you.

10. Remember Why You Started

Whether it's for your family, future, or simply peace of mind, always remember your "why."

Insight:

Debt is like an annoying mosquito. It keeps buzzing until you finally decide to slap it for good.

Mindset Shift:

Every time you make a smart financial decision; you're taking one more step toward freedom. Stay focused on the bigger picture.

Final Word

A debt-free mindset isn't about deprivation; it's about prioritisation. Think of it as a gym for your wallet—discipline now, flex later. And remember, every rupee saved is a step closer to the sweet, sweet freedom of not owing anyone anything.

Ready to make debt freedom your new normal? Go ahead, *you've got this!*

* * * * *

Chapter 6

Investing in Yourself: The Best ROI You'll Ever Get

Boosting Your Income Potential: Turn Your Skills and Hobbies into a Happiness Ticket

Let's get real for a moment. We all have something we're good at—yes, even you! Whether it's singing in the shower, draping sarees like a pro, or being the neighbourhood go-to person for tech help, every skill can be a goldmine. Now, imagine turning those talents into a side hustle that not only fills your pockets but also gives you joy. Sounds like a dream, right? Let's make it a reality.

1. Upskilling with Heart: The Key for Young Professionals

Upskilling isn't just for seasoned workers trying to stay relevant; it's a game-changer for young professionals too. Think of it as planting seeds for a future you'll thank yourself for.

- **Why Upskilling Matters?** In today's competitive world, a degree is only your entry ticket. Skills like coding, public speaking, digital marketing, or even emotional intelligence can set you apart.

- **How to upskill?**

    o Identify skills your dream job demands. Check LinkedIn profiles of people in roles you aspire to.

- o Take affordable online courses on platforms like Coursera, Udemy, or Skill share. Many offer free trials or certifications.

- **How to pick the right skill for you?**

  - o Be Future-Focused: Technology and trends change rapidly. Pick skills in emerging fields like data science, AI, or green energy.

  - o Develop Soft Skills: Communication, leadership, and adaptability are just as important as technical knowledge.

Pro Tip for Young Professionals: Think of upskilling as a Netflix subscription. Dedicate just an hour or two a week to learn something new. Over time, these "episodes" will add up to a life-changing series.

2. Kitchen Gardening: From Backyard to Business

Kitchen gardening is more than a stress-reliever – it's a business opportunity!

Story Time: Seema, a homemaker in Pune, started growing herbs and vegetables on her balcony. Her neighbours noticed the lush basil, mint, and cherry tomatoes and began asking for fresh produce. Seema turned her hobby into a small venture, selling potted herbs and "fresh-from-the-garden" veggies. Today, her monthly income from this hobby is ₹15,000, and she swears she's never felt closer to nature.

How to Start:

- Begin with easy-to-grow herbs like mint, coriander, and basil.

- Use social media to showcase your plants and offer gardening tips.
- Sell potted plants, fresh produce, or even homemade organic fertilisers.

3. Catering for Kitty Parties: Cook Your Way to Success

Do you love cooking? Here's a tasty idea: offer catering services for small events.

Story Time: Kavita, a stay-at-home mom from Jaipur, loved experimenting in the kitchen. Her friends raved about her chaat and desserts during kitty parties. One day, they insisted that she cater their next meet-up. Encouraged by their response, Kavita started a catering service exclusively for kitty parties. Now, she caters to 3–4 parties a month, earning ₹20,000–₹25,000—all while doing what she loves.

How to Start:

- Offer sample dishes to friends and family.
- Start with small, manageable gatherings like kitty parties or birthdays.
- Use WhatsApp groups for promotions and word-of-mouth marketing.

4. Aroma Candle Making: Let Your Creativity Shine

If you have a flair for creativity and love fragrances, why not try aroma candle making?

Story Time: Rohini, a graphic designer in Bengaluru, wanted a relaxing hobby. She started making candles for fun, using natural wax and essential oils. A friend suggested selling them at local flea markets. Within a year, Rohini was running an Instagram store and fulfilling bulk orders for wedding gifts. Her once-hobby now generates ₹40,000 a month.

How to Start:

- Experiment with scents like lavender, vanilla, or citrus.
- Invest in basic candle-making supplies.
- Use Instagram and marketplaces like Etsy to sell your creations.

5. Meditation Classes Online: Spread Peace, Earn Income

With mental health awareness growing, meditation classes are in high demand.

Story Time: Rajesh, an IT professional, struggled with work stress and found solace in meditation. Realising its transformative power, he got certified in mindfulness techniques. He started conducting online meditation sessions via Zoom, charging ₹500 per session. Within six months, Rajesh had a loyal clientele, earning an additional ₹25,000 monthly—and inspiring peace in others.

How to Start:

- Take a certification course in meditation or mindfulness.
- Begin with free trial sessions to build a client base.
- Offer personalised classes for individuals or groups.

6. Turn Hobbies into Hustles: A Win-Win

We all have hobbies that make us smile—why not let them make us money, too?

- **Voice Dubbing:** Got a great voice? Audiobooks and YouTube channels are booming markets.

- **Helping Neighbours:** Love working with people? Offer elderly care, running errands, or even driving them to appointments.

- **Fitness Freaks:** Start as a part-time yoga or Zumba instructor.

Pro Tip: When your side hustle is something you enjoy, it feels less like work and more like therapy—plus, you earn!

7. Building Passive Income: Let Your Skills Work for You

Passive income isn't just for stock market wizards. You can build it by sharing what you love.

- **Create Digital Products:** Write an e-book, design templates, or create a video course.

- **Start a Blog or YouTube Channel:** Share your journey—whether it's fitness, food, or finance. Ads and sponsorships will follow.

- **Sell Online:** Are you good at crafts, baking, or gardening? Start small, even on WhatsApp groups, and expand to platforms like Amazon or Etsy.

8. Time Management: Balancing Work and Passion

We all juggle busy lives, but trust me; you can carve out time for things you love.

- **Start Small:** Dedicate 1–2 hours a week to your hustle. As it grows, adjust your schedule.

- **Use Tools:** Apps like Notion or Google Calendar can help you organise tasks.

- **Set Boundaries:** Avoid burnout by giving yourself "me-time" every week.

9. Your Mindset: The Most Important Tool

Success begins with how you think. Believe in yourself and your unique abilities.

- **Embrace Your Talent:** Don't downplay your skills. The world needs what you have to offer.

- **Learn Along the Way:** You don't need to be perfect from day one. Start messy and improve as you go.

- **Stay Positive:** Challenges will come, but keep going. Every step forward is progress.

A Quick Wrap-Up

1. Discover what you're good at—be it gardening, cooking, or meditation—and enjoy doing.

2. Turn hobbies into side hustles with stories of joy and success.

3. Build passive income through digital products or online selling.

4. Network to spread the word and grow your audience.

5. Believe in your unique skills and start today.

Final Thought: Your hobbies and passions aren't just hobbies – they're happiness tickets waiting to be cashed. Whether it's growing herbs, creating candles, or teaching meditation, there's someone out there who needs what you offer. Why not start today? Your future self will thank you.

Physical and Mental Health: The Foundation for Sustained Financial Growth

As a doctor who has seen the human body and mind work tirelessly, I can confidently say your health is your most important investment. Without it, even the best financial plans can crumble like a house of cards. Let's explore how physical and mental health lay the foundation for sustained financial growth, supported by evidence, simple strategies, and a dash of inspiration.

The Health-Finance Connection

Here's the deal: poor health can drain your finances faster than an impulsive online shopping spree during a sale. The WHO estimates that non-communicable diseases (like diabetes and heart conditions) cost global economies **$47 trillion** from 2011 to 2030. For individuals, chronic illnesses can lead to loss of productivity, frequent medical bills, and even early retirement.

A study by the **American Heart Association** found that every dollar spent on preventive care saves about **$3.27** in healthcare costs. In simple terms, spending on your health today is like investing in a high-return mutual fund – it pays dividends.

Why Physical Health Matters for Wealth

Imagine your body as a machine. If poorly maintained, it breaks down and slows your productivity, focus, and income potential. Here's why physical health matters:

1. **Productivity and Earnings**

    A study in the **Journal of Occupational and Environmental Medicine** revealed that healthier employees are 25% more productive. More productivity can lead to better career growth, promotions, and financial stability.

2. **Medical Expenses**

   A person with obesity spends **$1,429 more annually** on healthcare than someone with a healthy weight, according to the CDC. Now think long-term: how much of your savings could be preserved with better health?

3. **Energy to Hustle**

   Whether it's running a startup, a side gig, or your household, physical fitness ensures you have the stamina to chase goals without burning out.

Mental Health and Financial Stability

Mental health is just as critical. Stress, anxiety, or depression can cloud judgement and lead to poor financial decisions—think impulsive purchases or procrastinating tax returns. According to **Deloitte**, poor mental health costs the Indian economy **₹1.1 trillion annually**, primarily due to reduced productivity.

Here's how mental health influences your finances:

1. **Better Decision-Making**

   A clear mind is your best financial advisor. Research shows that people with good mental health are more likely to save regularly and avoid debt traps.

2. **Workplace Performance**

   Companies like Google and TCS are investing in employee wellness because mental health boosts focus and creativity, leading to higher outputs and, in turn, better pay checks.

3. **Reduced Medical Costs**

Stress-related illnesses, from migraines to hypertension, can pile up hospital bills. Tackling mental health proactively can save significant money.

Simple Strategies for a Healthier, Wealthier You

Here's how to keep your health in check without overwhelming yourself or your wallet:

1. **Move More, Sit Less**

Walking for just 30 minutes a day can reduce your risk of heart disease by **35%** and diabetes by **40%**. Plus, it costs nothing!

2. **Eat Smart**

Replace processed foods with wholesome options. Local produce such as millets, lentils, and fresh vegetables are affordable and nutrient-packed.

3. **Sleep is Non-Negotiable**

Research in the journal **Sleep** shows that people who sleep less than 6 hours a night are 30% more likely to have financial difficulties due to health issues.

4. **Budget for Wellness**

Allocate a portion of your budget to fitness classes, therapy, or annual check-ups. Think of it as an SIP (Systematic Investment Plan) for your health.

5. **Mindfulness Practices**

Meditation and yoga don't just reduce stress; they improve your focus, helping you better track spending and investments.

The Bigger Picture

As the great Mahatma Gandhi said, "It is health that is real wealth and not pieces of gold and silver." By prioritising your well-being, you ensure that you have the energy, clarity, and resilience to build and sustain financial growth.

A Final Thought

Think of your health as the foundation of a skyscraper. The higher you aim, the stronger the base must be. So, take small, consistent steps toward better physical and mental health. Your bank account—and future self—will thank you.

By investing in your body and mind, you're not just avoiding medical expenses—you're unlocking your potential to earn, save, and grow wealth sustainably. Now, isn't that the kind of ROI everyone wants?

Time Management: Balancing Growth, Income, and Personal Well-Being

The True Value of "I Love You"

Picture this: Ravish, a hardworking doctor, often skipped family dinners to stay late at the clinic. On their 10th anniversary, his wife Sita told him, "Ravish, I don't need diamonds or a fancy dinner. I need you to look me in the eye and tell me you love me." He realised that while he provided financially, he had neglected the wealth of his presence. That evening, they sat on the balcony, with no fancy dinner and no expensive wine—just heartfelt words. And that became their best anniversary yet.

💡 *Lesson*: A hug and "I love you" are far more nourishing than a five-star meal. Fancy restaurants can wait. Relationships cannot.

Gadgets Can't Replace a Game of Catch

Anil, a tech enthusiast dad, bought his son the latest gaming console, hoping to see his face light up. But his son remained glued to the screen, distant and distracted. One Sunday, Anil left his phone behind, grabbed a cricket bat, and asked his son to join him in the park. The sound of laughter, running footsteps, and a cleanly struck six was music to his ears. His son said, "Dad, this is more fun than any game on the console!"

💡 *Lesson*: Kids may ask for gadgets, but their hearts crave your time. Invest in memories, not machinery.

Well-Being on the Path to Wealth

Chasing wealth without health is like climbing a mountain only to realise there's no oxygen at the top. Remember, success is hollow if your body is too tired or your mind too restless to enjoy it.

Quotes to Remember:

- "He who has health has hope; and he who has hope has everything." – Arabian Proverb

- "Wealth is the ability to fully experience life." – Henry David Thoreau

Prioritise well-being:

- Block time for yoga, meditation, or a morning walk.

- Set boundaries for work hours. Your inbox will still be there tomorrow.

What People Regret on Their Deathbed

Bronnie Ware, a nurse who worked in palliative care, recorded common regrets of the dying:

1. *"I wish I had spent more time with loved ones."*

2. *"I wish I hadn't worked so hard."*

3. *"I wish I'd let myself be happier."*

How to Avoid These Regrets:

- Set non-negotiable family time.

- Pursue hobbies that make you smile.

- Practice gratitude for what you have today.

Don't Let Money Hijack Your Happiness

Money is a tool, not the destination. It buys comfort and freedom but can't fill a void in your soul. Don't become the honeybee that never drinks its honey. You can't take a fat bank balance to your grave, but you can leave a legacy of love and impact.

Make Money Work for You, Not Against You:

- Use wealth to spend time with family, not to substitute for it.

- Prioritise experiences over material possessions.

- Share your blessings by helping others in need.

A Simple Reminder

On your journey to growth and wealth, remember: **Time, love, and health are the real currencies.** Earn them, invest in them, and spend them wisely.

And as you sit with your family tonight, put your phone away, hold their hands, and say, "I'm here for you." That moment will be priceless—far more valuable than any pay check.

Establishing Safety Nets for Life: Why Every Rupee You Save Can Save You

Life is unpredictable. One day, it's all smiles, and the next, you could be facing a storm you never saw coming. That's why building financial safety nets—like a **6-month emergency fund, health insurance**, and **term insurance**—is crucial. These are not just financial tools but lifeboats that protect your dreams, dignity, and your loved ones' future when life gets tough.

Let me take you on a journey to understand their importance, not just in numbers but in the emotional impact they can have.

1. Emergency Fund: Your Financial First Aid

An emergency fund is like your financial first aid kit. It's not for vacations or fancy gadgets; it's for when life suddenly flips the script – a job loss, medical emergency, or a leaky roof right before the monsoon.

How Much Should You Save?

- The goal is **6 months' worth of essential expenses**. This includes rent/EMI, groceries, utilities, transportation, medical costs, and school fees.
- If your monthly expense is ₹50,000, you should aim for ₹3,00,000.

Where to Park This Money?

Your emergency fund should be **safe, accessible, and low-risk:**

- **Savings Account:** For instant access.
- **Liquid Mutual Funds:** Offers slightly higher returns while being relatively liquid.

- **Short-Term Fixed Deposits:** Can work if you don't need immediate access.

Start Small, Think Big

Building an emergency fund takes time. Start by saving ₹10,000 or 1 month's expenses and build up gradually. Remember, every rupee counts.

2. Health Insurance: Guarding Against Medical Disasters

Imagine being hospitalised for a week and handed a ₹5 lakh bill at discharge. Without health insurance, that bill can wipe out years of savings in an instant. Healthcare costs in India are soaring, and a good health insurance policy can save you from such financial devastation.

How to Choose the Right Health Insurance?

1. **Coverage Amount:**

   o **Individuals:** Start with ₹5–10 lakhs.

   o **Families (2 adults + 2 kids):** ₹10–20 lakhs, especially in metros where medical costs are steep.

2. **Key Features to Look For:**

   o **Cashless Network:** Check if your preferred hospitals are in the insurer's network.

   o **Room Rent Limits:** Avoid plans with restrictive room rent caps.

   o **No Claim Bonus (NCB):** Opt for plans that increase your coverage for every claim-free year.

   o **Day-Care Coverage:** Modern treatments often don't require 24-hour hospitalisation. Ensure your plan covers these.

3. **Critical Illness Rider:** Adds coverage for major illnesses like cancer or heart conditions.

Ideal Premium and Coverage

- Premiums are affordable if you start early. A 30-year-old can get ₹10 lakh coverage for around ₹12,000–₹20,000 annually.

3. Term Insurance: The Ultimate Gift of Security

Term insurance is love wrapped in financial planning. It doesn't benefit you directly, but it ensures your family's dreams live on, even if you're not there.

How to Choose the Right Term Insurance?

1. **Coverage Amount:**

   o Choose a cover of **15–20 times your annual income**.

   o If you earn ₹10 lakhs a year, go for a ₹1.5–2 crore cover.

2. **Policy Term:**

   o Ideally, until your retirement age (60–65 years).

   o If you're 30 now, choose a 30–35-year term.

3. **Insurer's Reputation:**

   o Look for insurers with a **Claim Settlement Ratio (CSR) above 95%**. It's a good indicator of their reliability in paying claims.

4. **Riders for Extra Protection:**

   o **Accidental Death Benefit:** Provides an extra payout if death occurs due to an accident.

- o **Critical Illness Cover:** Provides a lump sum if diagnosed with a critical illness.

Ideal Premium and Coverage

For a healthy 30-year-old, a ₹1 crore cover costs around ₹6,000–₹10,000 annually. This is one of the most affordable ways to secure your family's financial future.

Harish's Wake-Up Call: A Story of Resilience

Harish was a 35-year-old schoolteacher, the sole breadwinner for his family of four. Life was stable, though not lavish. His wife managed the home, their elder daughter was preparing for her board exams, and their younger son was in primary school.

Harish always thought, "Why should I worry? I'm healthy, I have a steady job, and we manage well." He had no emergency fund, no health insurance, and no term insurance.

One fateful evening, while returning home, Harish met with an accident. He survived, but his injuries required surgery and a month-long hospital stay. The total bill? ₹8 lakhs. Without health insurance, Harish had to borrow money from friends, liquidate his modest savings, and even take an emergency loan at a high interest rate.

The financial strain didn't end there. Unable to work for 3 months, Harish found himself juggling debts while trying to pay school fees and EMIs. The entire family felt the impact—his daughter's tuition was postponed, and his wife sold her jewellery to meet daily expenses.

This experience was a turning point for Harish. Over the next year, he:

1. Built a **₹3 lakh emergency fund**, saving systematically every month.

2. Purchased a **₹15 lakh family health insurance policy** with critical illness cover.

3. Bought **term insurance worth ₹2 crore** to secure his family's future.

Today, Harish breathes easily. He says, "I can't predict life's storms, but now I know I'm ready for them."

Why You Need These Safety Nets

Think of these financial tools as your invisible bodyguards:

- **Emergency Fund:** Covers your back when income stops or expenses spike unexpectedly.

- **Health Insurance:** Prevents you from turning a health crisis into a financial crisis.

- **Term Insurance:** Ensures your family's dreams don't shatter in your absence.

Final Thought

Don't wait for a Harish-like moment to wake up. Building safety nets is not about pessimism; it's about responsibility. It's about giving your family a life of dignity, even when things go wrong. Start small, but start today. Because life may not come with guarantees, but your finances can.

Tax Optimisation in India: A Detailed Guide (As of Feb – 2025)

Tax optimisation is not about avoiding taxes but strategically planning your finances to reduce your tax liability within the boundaries of the law. In India, the Income Tax Act, 1961 provides several avenues to optimise taxes and the latest **Finance Bill, 2025**, introduces key updates. Let's explore them step by step:

1. Understand Your Tax Regime

India has two tax regimes:

- **Old Tax Regime**: Offers exemptions and deductions under various sections like 80C, 80D, etc.

- **New Tax Regime**: Lower tax rates but without most exemptions and deductions.

  Pro Tip: Compare both regimes each year to choose the one most beneficial for you. Use online calculators for a quick comparison.

  UPDATE: In the **Union Budget 2025**, Finance Minister Nirmala Sitharaman announced significant reforms to the **New Tax Regime**, aiming to provide substantial relief to the middle class and stimulate economic growth.

Key Highlights:

1. **Tax Exemption Limit Increased:**

   o The income threshold for tax exemption under the new tax regime has been raised to **₹12 lakh** from the previous ₹7 lakh.

2. **Standard Deduction:**

   o A standard deduction of ₹**75,000** is available for salaried individuals.

3. **Revised Tax Slabs:**

   o The new tax slabs under the revised regime are as follows:

Annual Income (₹)	Tax Rate
Up to 4,00,000	Nil
4,00,001 – 8,00,000	5%
8,00,001 – 12,00,000	10%
12,00,001 – 16,00,000	15%
16,00,001 – 20,00,000	20%
20,00,001 – 24,00,000	25%
Above 24,00,000	30%

Implications:

- **For Salaried Individuals:**

  o With the standard deduction of ₹75,000, salaried individuals earning up to ₹**12.75 lakh** annually will not be liable to pay any income tax under the new regime.

2. Use Section 80C (₹1.5 Lakh Limit)

This is the most popular section for tax-saving investments. Some eligible options include:

- **Employee Provident Fund (EPF):** Automatically deducted if you are salaried.

- **Public Provident Fund (PPF)**: Long-term investment with tax-free returns.

- **Equity Linked Savings Scheme (ELSS)**: Tax-saving mutual funds with a lock-in of 3 years.

- **National Savings Certificate (NSC)**: Government-backed fixed return scheme.

- **Tax-saving Fixed Deposits**: Lock-in of 5 years, but interest is taxable.

- **Principal Repayment of Home Loan**: Eligible for deduction under 80C.

- **Life Insurance Premiums**: Ensure the annual premium is less than 10% of the sum assured.

Pro Tip: If you're unsure where to start, PPF and ELSS are great options for beginners.

3. Maximise Section 80D (Health Insurance)

- Premiums for health insurance qualify for deduction:

  - Up to ₹25,000 for self, spouse, and children.

  - Additional ₹50,000 for senior citizen parents.

Example: If you're paying ₹20,000 for your family and ₹35,000 for your senior citizen parents, you can claim ₹55,000.

4. Use Home Loan Deductions

- **Section 24(b)**: Claim up to ₹2 lakh on interest paid on your home loan (self-occupied property).

- **Section 80EE/80EEA**: Additional deduction of ₹50,000 or ₹1.5 lakh for first-time homebuyers.

Pro Tip: Joint home loans allow both borrowers to claim these deductions individually, effectively doubling the tax benefit.

5. Leverage NPS Contributions (National Pension Scheme)

- Section 80CCD (1): Contributions up to ₹1.5 lakh are covered under 80C.

- Section 80CCD (1B): Additional deduction of ₹50,000 for NPS contributions.

- Section 80CCD (2): Employer contributions up to 10% of your salary are tax-free and do not count under the ₹1.5 lakh 80C limit.

6. Claim Rent Deductions

- **Salaried Employees with HRA**: House Rent Allowance (HRA) is partially or fully tax-free based on rent paid.

- **Self-employed/No HRA**: Claim deduction under Section 80GG for rent paid (subject to conditions).

Pro Tip: Maintain rent receipts and lease agreements as proof.

7. Save on Long-term Investments

Investments in long-term capital gains (LTCG) can help optimise taxes:

- **Stocks and Equity Mutual Funds**: LTCG up to ₹1 lakh is tax-free.

- **Real Estate**: Invest in another property or capital gains bonds (Section 54EC) to avoid taxes on gains.

8. Claim Work-related Deductions

- **Standard Deduction**: ₹50,000 is automatically deducted for salaried individuals.

- **Professional Tax**: Deductible if paid by you or your employer.

9. Use Tax-free Perquisites and Allowances

Ask your employer to structure your salary with tax-free components such as:

- Food coupons/vouchers (₹50 per meal).
- LTA (Leave Travel Allowance): Exempt for travel within India.
- Education allowance: ₹100 per child per month.

10. Tax Planning for Freelancers/Professionals

- Use **Section 44ADA**: Under the presumptive taxation scheme, only 50% of your gross receipts are taxable if turnover is under ₹50 lakh.
- Deduct business expenses like rent, utilities, and software tools.

11. Donate and Save

- Donations to specified funds/charities under Section 80G are deductible.
- Ensure the organisation has a valid 80G certificate.

12. Invest in Tax-efficient Instruments

Some investments offer tax-free returns:

- PPF, Sukanya Samriddhi Yojana, and EPF.
- Tax-free bonds issued by government organisations.

13. Capitalise on Agricultural Income

Agricultural income is fully exempt from tax. If you have a family property with agricultural activities, use this to your advantage.

14. Avoid Common Pitfalls

- **Avoid Last-minute Investments**: Plan at the start of the financial year.

- **Check Lock-in Periods**: Some instruments, like PPF and ELSS, have lock-ins.

- **Diversify Investments**: Don't put all your savings into one option like insurance policies.

15. Seek Professional Advice

If your income sources or financial situation is complex, consider consulting a Chartered Accountant (CA). A CA can help you:

- File returns accurately.
- Avoid notices from the Income Tax Department.
- Maximise deductions and exemptions.

Tax Optimisation Example: Comparing Old and New Tax Regimes

Here's how the tax liability differs between the **Old Tax Regime** (with deductions) and the **New Tax Regime** (lower tax rates but no deductions) for two income levels: **₹12 LPA (employee)** and **₹36 LPA (professional).**

1. Employee with ₹12 LPA Income (FY 2025-26)

Assumptions:

- Standard deduction: ₹50,000 (Old Regime); ₹75,000 (New regime)
- Investment in Section 80C (PPF, EPF, etc.): ₹1.5 lakh
- Health insurance premium (Section 80D): ₹25,000
- Housing loan interest (Section 24B): ₹1 lakh

Old Tax Regime:

Gross Income: ₹12,00,000

Deductions:

- Standard Deduction: ₹50,000
- 80C: ₹1,50,000
- 80D: ₹25,000
- Section 24B (Interest on home loan): ₹1,00,000
- **Total Deductions:** ₹3,25,000

Taxable Income: ₹12,00,000 − ₹3,25,000 = ₹8,75,000

Tax Calculation:

- 0–₹2,50,000: Nil
- ₹2,50,001–₹2,75,000: 5% = ₹1,250

Tax Payable: ₹1,250

New Tax Regime:

Gross Income: ₹12,00,000

₹75,000 standard Deduction Allowed

- Tax Calculation: For **salaried individuals,** after applying the standard deduction, the **effective tax-free income limit is ₹12.75 lakh**.

Example Calculation:

- **Gross Annual Income**: ₹13,00,000
- **Less: Standard Deduction**: ₹75,000
- **Net Taxable Income**: ₹12,25,000

Since the net taxable income of ₹12,25,000 is below the ₹12,75,000 threshold, the individual would **not be liable to pay any income tax** under the new regime.

Tax Comparison: Old vs. New Regime for a Professional with ₹36 LPA (FY 2025-26)

With the latest **Union Budget 2025** updates, let's compare the tax liability for a **professional earning ₹36,00,000 per annum** under both tax regimes.

◉ Scenario 1: New Tax Regime (2025-26)

- **Only Standard Deduction of ₹75,000 allowed**
- **Revised tax slabs apply**

Tax Calculation Under New Regime

Income Component	Amount (₹)
Gross Salary	36,00,000
Standard Deduction	(-) 75,000
Taxable Income	35,25,000

Tax Slab (New Regime)	Tax Rate	Tax Payable
Up to ₹4,00,000	0%	₹0
₹4,00,001 – ₹8,00,000	5%	₹20,000
₹8,00,001 – ₹12,00,000	10%	₹40,000
₹12,00,001 – ₹16,00,000	15%	₹60,000
₹16,00,001 – ₹20,00,000	20%	₹80,000
₹20,00,001 – ₹24,00,000	25%	₹1,00,000
₹24,00,001 – ₹35,25,000	30%	₹3,37,500

Total Tax (Before Cess) = ₹6,37,500

- **Health & Education Cess (4%) = ₹25,500**
- **Final Tax Payable = ₹6,63,000**

◉ Scenario 2: Old Tax Regime (2025-26)

- **Deductions available under 80C, 80D, NPS, and Home Loan Interest**
- **Higher taxable income reduction possible**

Assumed Deductions (For a Professional)

Section	Deduction Claimed
Standard Deduction	₹50,000
Section 80C (PPF, ELSS, EPF, LIC, etc.)	₹1,50,000
Section 80D (Health Insurance Premium)	₹50,000
NPS Contribution (Section 80CCD(1B))	₹50,000
Home Loan Interest (Sec 24b, if applicable)	₹2,00,000

Tax Calculation Under Old Regime

Income Component	Amount (₹)
Gross Salary	36,00,000
Total Deductions	(-) 5,00,000
Taxable Income	31,00,000

Tax Slab (Old Regime)	Tax Rate	Tax Payable
Up to ₹2,50,000	0%	₹0
₹2,50,001 – ₹5,00,000	5%	₹12,500
₹5,00,001 – ₹10,00,000	20%	₹1,00,000
₹10,00,001 – ₹31,00,000	30%	₹6,30,000

Total Tax (Before Cess) = ₹7,42,500

- Health & Education Cess (4%) = ₹29,700
- Final Tax Payable = ₹7,72,200

📌 Final Comparison

Income Level	Old Regime Tax (₹)	New Regime Tax (₹)	Best Option
₹36 LPA (Professional)	₹7,72,200	₹6,63,000	New Regime

✅ **Verdict:** The **New Tax Regime is better** (₹1,09,200 lower tax) for a professional with ₹36 LPA **if deductions are limited**.

Summary of Tax Payable:

Income Level	Old Regime Tax Payable	New Regime Tax Payable	Best Regime
₹12 LPA (Employee)	₹1,250	₹0	New
₹36 LPA (Professional)	₹7,72,500	₹6,63,500	New

Key Insight:

Choosing the regime depends on your deductions. Evaluate both options annually for the best tax outcome.

Conclusion

Tax optimisation is not a one-time task. It requires regular evaluation of your financial situation and alignment with your goals. By choosing the right mix of instruments, planning your investments early, and leveraging all deductions, you can significantly reduce your tax outgo and use the savings to grow wealth. After all, why give away more money to the taxman than necessary when you can legally keep it for yourself?

* * * * *

PART 03

WEALTH CREATION – INVESTMENTS, FIRE, AND PORTFOLIO MANAGEMENT

Chapter 7

Investments: Building Your Wealth Toolbox

Investing can seem like a labyrinth, but it's simpler than you think when you break it down. This chapter unpacks traditional and modern investment options, explains the crucial balance of risk vs. reward, and emphasises the power of compounding—all essential tools for building your financial health. Let's start from the foundation and work our way up.

Traditional Options: The Cornerstone of Indian Savings

Fixed Deposits (FDs): A Safe Haven

FDs are one of the most popular and straightforward investment options in India. They offer:

- **Guaranteed Returns**: Fixed interest rates ensure your returns are predictable.

- **Low Risk**: Ideal for risk-averse individuals.

- **Liquidity**: Some flexibility to withdraw, though premature withdrawals incur penalties.

Real-Life Story: Ravi, a retired schoolteacher, invested his savings in FDs for over 30 years. While his returns didn't grow significantly, he never lost sleep over market fluctuations. "Safety first," he would always say, proving FDs are a go-to option for peace of mind.

Drawbacks:

- Returns often struggle to beat inflation.
- Less tax-efficient unless you opt for tax-saving FDs under Section 80C.

Recurring Deposits (RDs): Disciplined Savings

RDs are perfect for those who want to invest small, consistent amounts monthly. They share benefits similar to FDs but encourage regular savings.

Real-Life Story: Meera, a young software engineer, started an RD to save for her brother's wedding. She consistently deposited ₹10,000 every month, accumulating ₹1.25 lakh in a year. This disciplined approach helped her fund a beautiful family celebration without debt.

Drawbacks:

- Slightly lower returns than FDs.
- Limited flexibility in withdrawal.

Public Provident Fund (PPF): A Long-Term Gem

PPF combines safety, attractive returns and tax benefits:

- **Tax-Efficient**: Returns are tax-free under Section 10(11).
- **Compounding Power**: A 15-year lock-in boosts returns.
- **Risk-Free**: Backed by the government.

Famous Quote: "Someone's sitting in the shade today because someone planted a tree a long time ago." – Warren Buffett. PPF works on this principle. Start early and enjoy financial shade later.

Limitations:

- Lock-in period restricts liquidity.

- Fixed interest rates may not match market-linked returns.

National Pension System (NPS): Retirement Planning Simplified

NPS is a government-backed pension scheme designed for retirement savings. Features include:

- **Dual Tax Benefits**: Deductions under Sections 80C and 80CCD.

- **Flexibility**: Choose between equity and debt exposure.

- **Annuity Post-Retirement**: Ensures lifelong income.

Real-life story: Shalini, a 40-year-old doctor, started contributing ₹20,000 annually to NPS. By the time she retired at 60, her corpus had grown to ₹1 crore. Her disciplined contributions ensured a steady pension during retirement.

Limitations:

- Partial withdrawals are allowed only after three years.

- Returns depend on fund performance.

Gold: Timeless Security

Indians have long cherished gold as both an ornament and an investment. Modern ways to invest include gold ETFs and sovereign gold bonds. Benefits include:

- **Hedge Against Inflation**: Gold tends to hold value during economic downturns.

- **Liquidity**: Easily convertible to cash.

Story: During the 2008 financial crisis, families holding physical gold weathered the storm better than those dependent on equities alone. Gold proved to be a true safe haven.

Risks:

- Price volatility in the short term.
- No interest or dividend income.

Modern Options: Stepping into the Market

Mutual Funds: Diverse and Accessible

Mutual funds pool money from various investors to invest in diversified assets such as equities, bonds, or a mix.

How to Choose the Right Mutual Fund:

1. **Low Expense Ratio**: A lower expense ratio means more of your returns stay in your pocket. Compare funds within the same category.
2. **Fund Performance**: Check consistent performance over 3, 5, and 10 years.
3. **Investment Objective**: Match the fund's objective with your financial goals.

Proposed Allocation Strategy:

- **50% in Index or Large-Cap Funds**: These offer stability and mirror the market.
- **30% in Mid-Cap Funds**: For higher growth potential.
- **20% in Small-Cap Funds**: High risk but potentially high returns.

Alternatively, allocate 50% to Flexi-Cap Funds to allow fund managers to optimise across market caps.

Why This Works Better Than Actively Managed Funds:

- Lower expense ratios for index funds.
- Avoids the risk of fund manager underperformance.
- Diversification across market segments reduces risk.

Statistics Challenges:

- Market-linked, so returns are not guaranteed.
- Expense ratios and exit loads can impact profits.

Thematic Funds: When to Invest

Thematic funds focus on specific sectors, such as healthcare, technology, or ESG (Environmental, Social, and Governance).

Guidelines for Investing:

- **Expertise Matters**: Invest only if you have deep knowledge of the sector. For example, as a doctor, you might spot trends in healthcare and invest confidently.
- **Long-Term Trends**: Choose themes with structural growth potential, not social media hype.
- **Diversify**: Limit exposure to 10-15% of your portfolio, as thematic funds carry concentrated risks.

Real-Life Example: Dr. Ramesh, a cardiologist, noticed a surge in demand for medical devices post-pandemic. He invested in a healthcare-themed mutual fund in 2020. By 2025, his investment doubled, showcasing how industry knowledge can give you an edge.

Caution Stocks: Ownership in Companies

Investing in stocks means owning a share in a company. Stocks offer:

- **High Returns**: Historically, equities have outperformed most asset classes over the long term.

- **Dividend Income**: An additional source of passive income.

Famous Quote: "In the short run, the market is a voting machine, but in the long run, it is a weighing machine." – Benjamin Graham. This underscores the importance of patience in stock investing.

How to Pick Stocks Wisely:

1. **Avoid Penny Stocks:**

   o Penny stocks may seem attractive due to their low prices but are often highly volatile and lack strong fundamentals. Instead, focus on established companies with proven track records.

2. **Don't Follow Market Hype:**

   o Be cautious of stocks trending on social media. Invest based on data and analysis, not FOMO (Fear of Missing Out).

3. **Understand Valuation:**

   o Learn to calculate intrinsic value using methods like Discounted Cash Flow (DCF) analysis or Price-to-Earnings (P/E) ratio comparisons.

4. **Know Market Caps:**

   o **Large-Cap Stocks**: Established, stable companies (e.g., TCS, HDFC). Suitable for low-risk investors aiming for consistent returns.

- o **Mid-Cap Stocks**: Growth-oriented companies (e.g., Apollo Hospitals). Offer higher growth potential with moderate risk.

- o **Small-Cap Stocks**: High-growth but volatile companies (e.g. Brightcom Group). These stocks can deliver significant returns but require thorough research and a higher risk tolerance.

5. **Key Ratios to Monitor**:

- o **P/E Ratio** (Price-to-Earnings Ratio): Shows how much investors are willing to pay per rupee of earnings. A lower P/E ratio compared to peers may indicate undervaluation. However, a very low P/E could signal trouble.

- o **Debt-to-Equity Ratio**: Measures the company's leverage. A ratio below 1 is generally considered healthy, indicating the company is not overly reliant on debt.

- o **Return on Equity (ROE)**: Indicates how efficiently the company uses shareholders' funds to generate profit. A consistent ROE above 15% is a good sign.

- o **Price-to-Book (P/B) Ratio**: Evaluates the company's market value relative to its book value. A P/B ratio below 1 may indicate undervaluation, but this is more useful for asset-heavy companies like banks.

- o **Current Ratio**: Measures liquidity. A ratio above 1 means the company can cover its short-term obligations.

- o **Earnings Per Share (EPS)**: Reflects the company's profitability on a per-share basis. Consistently growing EPS is a positive indicator.

6. **Analyse Financial Statements**:

   o **Balance Sheet**: Understand assets, liabilities, and equity. High debt and low cash reserves are red flags.

   o **Profit & Loss Statement**: Look for consistent revenue and profit growth over the years. Declining revenues or shrinking margins can signal trouble.

   o **Cash Flow Statement**: Ensure the company generates positive cash flow from operations, not just financing or investing activities. Positive operational cash flow shows that the company's core business is profitable.

Apollo Hospitals: A Case Study in Stock Analysis

Overview Balance Sheet Analysis:

- **Assets**: Steady growth in tangible assets like hospitals and equipment.

- **Liabilities**: Moderate debt-to-equity ratio (~0.7), indicating manageable leverage.

- **Cash Reserves**: Healthy cash reserves, ensuring liquidity for expansion plans.

Profit & Loss Statement:

- **Revenue Growth**: Annual revenue has shown a consistent growth rate of 15% over the past five years, driven by increased patient volumes and specialised treatments.

- **Profit Margins**: Net profit margins are around 8-10%, reflecting efficient cost management despite the capital-intensive nature of healthcare.

Cash Flow Statement:

- **Operating Cash Flow**: Positive cash flow from operations due to high patient turnover and strong billing systems.

- **Investment Activities**: Funds reinvested in expanding facilities and acquiring advanced medical technologies.

Ratios:

- **P/E Ratio**: At ~40, higher than peers, reflecting market confidence in growth potential.

- **ROE**: ~18%, showcasing efficient use of equity to generate profits.

- **Debt-to-Equity**: 0.7, indicating balanced use of leverage.

Insights:

- Apollo Hospitals stands out due to its market leadership and focus on innovation in healthcare.

- Long-term investors benefit from its consistent revenue growth and ability to adapt to healthcare trends.

Exchange-Traded Funds (ETFs): The Hybrid Option

ETFs are like mutual funds, but they trade on stock exchanges like individual stocks. They are versatile investment tools that offer the following:

1. **Low Cost**: ETFs typically have lower expense ratios compared to actively managed mutual funds. This means more of your returns stay in your pocket.

2. **Flexibility**: ETFs can be bought or sold throughout the trading day, unlike mutual funds, which are priced only at the end of the day.

3. **Diversification**: By tracking an index or a basket of assets, ETFs reduce the risk of poor performance from a single stock.

Types of ETFs:

- **Index ETFs**: Track major indices like Nifty 50 or Sensex. Ideal for broad market exposure with minimal effort.

- **Sectoral/Thematic ETFs**: Focus on specific sectors like technology, healthcare, or renewable energy.

- **Gold ETFs**: Allow investors to gain exposure to gold without holding physical gold.

- **Bond ETFs**: Invest in government or corporate bonds suitable for conservative investors.

- **International ETFs**: Provide exposure to global markets, enabling diversification beyond domestic stocks.

- **ESG ETFs**: Focus on companies meeting environmental, social, and governance criteria.

How ETFs Mitigate Risk Compared to Individual Stocks:

- **Built-In Diversification**: An ETF holding 50-100 stocks spreads the risk, reducing the impact of any single underperforming stock.

- **Lower Volatility**: Broad exposure to an index smoothens the sharp movements often seen in individual stocks.

- **Passive Management**: Since ETFs track indices, they eliminate the risk of poor fund manager decisions.

Example

Who Should Invest in ETFs?

- Beginners who want a simple, low-cost entry into equity markets.

- Investors looking for broad market exposure.

- Those seeking diversification without actively managing a portfolio.

Concerns:

- Requires a demat account for trading.

- Tracking errors can occasionally lead to minor deviations from the index performance.

A Simple Guide to Unlisted Shares, IPOs, and Cryptocurrencies

1. Unlisted Shares

Unlisted shares are the shares of companies that are not traded on stock exchanges like NSE or BSE. These are usually companies in their early growth stage or private companies that haven't gone public yet.

- Pros:

    o Potential for high returns if the company grows.

    o Access to early-stage investment opportunities.

- Cons:

    o Highly illiquid – you can't sell them as easily as listed shares.

    o Limited transparency and regulatory oversight.

Caution:

Unlisted shares are like laddoos. Sweet, but if you overdo it without proper understanding, it may upset your financial stomach. Only invest if you thoroughly research or consult a professional.

2. IPOs (Initial Public Offerings)

IPOs are when a private company goes public by offering its shares to the general public for the first time. It's like the company's grand debut on the stock market stage!

- Pros:

    o Opportunity to invest in a company at its growth stage.

- o Can yield good short-term listing gains or long-term growth.

- Cons:

   - o IPOs can be overhyped, with prices set at premium valuations.

   - o Not every IPO is a winner; some end up underperforming.

Caution:

Don't get carried away by IPO fever. It's like the first day of a blockbuster movie – lots of buzz, but not every movie turns out to be a hit. Do your homework before buying tickets!

3. Cryptocurrencies

Imagine this: you have ₹500 in your pocket. You can buy a snack, pay for a bus ride, or save it in your piggy bank. Now, what if this ₹500 existed only on your phone or computer as a string of numbers and not as physical cash? That's basically what a cryptocurrency is—a type of money that exists only digitally, on the internet.

Let's break it down step by step so it's crystal clear.

What Are Cryptocurrencies?

Cryptocurrencies are digital or virtual currencies that don't exist as coins or notes but as data stored on a special kind of database called a blockchain.

- **Example:** Bitcoin, Ethereum, Dogecoin (yes, that started as a joke!).

Unlike regular money like rupees or dollars, cryptocurrencies aren't controlled by governments or banks. Instead, they're decentralised, which means a large network of computers worldwide manages them.

Think of it like a huge online notebook where every single transaction is written down and checked by thousands of computers to ensure no one cheats. This notebook is the blockchain, and it's what makes cryptocurrencies secure.

How Do Cryptocurrencies Work?

When you buy, sell or trade cryptocurrency, you're essentially moving digital money from one online wallet (yours) to another.

- **Online Wallets:** These are apps or platforms where your cryptocurrency is stored, like Paytm or Google Pay, but for crypto.

- **Transactions:** Say you want to pay your friend in Bitcoin. Your transaction gets verified by computers (called miners) on the blockchain to ensure it's legit, and once verified, it's added to the blockchain for everyone to see.

You can also buy cryptocurrencies on platforms called **crypto exchanges**, like Binance, Coinbase, or WazirX. These work a bit like stock markets – you buy when prices are low and sell when prices are high to make a profit.

Why Are Cryptocurrencies Popular?

1. **No Middleman:** No banks or governments are involved. Transactions go directly from person to person.

2. **Global Use:** You can send money anywhere in the world instantly without worrying about currency exchange rates or fees.

3. **Privacy:** You don't need to share personal information like your name or account number for transactions.

4. **Potential to Grow:** Some people have made a lot of money investing in cryptocurrencies because their value can skyrocket.

Pros of Cryptocurrencies

- **Fast Transactions:** No waiting days for bank transfers; crypto transactions are usually quick.

- **Secure:** The blockchain system is very hard to hack or cheat.

- **Access for Everyone:** Anyone with a smartphone and internet can use crypto, even if they don't have a bank account.

- **High Returns (Sometimes):** If you invest wisely, cryptocurrencies can multiply your money.

Cons of Cryptocurrencies

- **Price Fluctuations:** Cryptocurrencies can go up or down in value *very quickly*. One day, Bitcoin is worth ₹40 lakhs; the next day, it's ₹30 lakhs.

- **Not Widely Accepted:** You can't use crypto everywhere. You can't buy pani puri with Bitcoin yet!

- **No Refunds:** If you send money to the wrong person or lose your password, there's no way to get it back.

- **Risk of Scams:** There are many fake crypto projects or exchanges that steal people's money.

Cautions Before Getting into Cryptocurrencies

1. **Start Small:** If you're investing, don't put all your savings into crypto. It's risky, so only invest money you can afford to lose.

2. **Do Your Research:** Always learn about the cryptocurrency and the platform before investing. Avoid anything that sounds "too good to be true."

3. **Use Trusted Platforms:** Only trade on well-known crypto exchanges.

4. **Keep Your Wallet Safe:** Write down your wallet passwords and backup codes in a secure place. If you lose them, your crypto is gone forever.

5. **Beware of Scams:** Don't fall for messages or emails promising to double your money or asking for your wallet details.

Should You Use or Invest in Cryptocurrencies?

Cryptocurrencies are exciting, no doubt. They're like the internet was in the early 2000s – new, confusing, and full of potential. But remember, they're also unpredictable. While some people have become millionaires from crypto, others have lost everything.

If you're curious, start small. Learn how it works, understand the risks, and never rush into it just because someone else is doing it. Cryptocurrencies might be the future, but handling them wisely today is the key.

Caution:

Investing in cryptocurrencies is like boarding a rollercoaster with no seatbelt. Thrilling? Yes. Safe? Not really. Only invest what you can afford to lose and keep your emotions in check.

Final Thoughts

All three – unlisted shares, IPOs, and cryptocurrencies – can be exciting but come with significant risks. Always remember the golden rule of investing: "Never put all your eggs in one basket." A diversified portfolio, thorough research, and a pinch of caution will keep your financial journey smoother and safer.

Disclaimer: This note is for educational purposes only and not financial advice. Invest wisely!

What Are REITs?

A Real Estate Investment Trust (REIT) is a company that owns, operates, or finances income-generating real estate. Think of it as a mutual fund for real estate. Instead of buying an apartment or office space, you invest in a REIT, which does all the heavy lifting of owning and managing properties.

REITs are popular among investors because they provide a way to earn regular income through dividends and long-term capital appreciation, all without needing to deal with tenants, maintenance, or property taxes.

Types of REITs

1. Equity REITs:

    o These invest directly in properties such as malls, apartments, or office buildings.

    o Revenue is earned primarily from renting these properties.

2. Mortgage REITs (mREITs):

    o These provide financing for real estate by purchasing or originating mortgages.

    o Income comes from the interest on these loans.

3. Hybrid REITs:

    o A mix of equity and mortgage REITs.

    o They earn from both rental income and interest.

How Do REITs Work?

- REITs pool money from multiple investors to purchase and manage large-scale real estate projects.

- By law, most REITs are required to pay at least 90% of their taxable income as dividends to shareholders.

- This makes REITs an attractive choice for income-focused investors.

Why Invest in REITs?

1. Diversification:

   o Adds exposure to real estate in your portfolio without direct property ownership.

2. Liquidity:

   o Unlike physical real estate, REITs are traded on stock exchanges. You can buy and sell them like stocks.

3. Regular Income:

   o REITs are known for paying consistent dividends, making them a favourite for retirees or those seeking passive income.

4. Professional Management:

   o Experienced managers handle property acquisition, leasing, and maintenance.

5. Tax Benefits:

   o In India, REITs are exempt from dividend distribution tax, making them tax-efficient for investors.

Risks of Investing in REITs

1. Market Volatility:

   o REITs are traded on exchanges, so their prices fluctuate like stocks.

2. Interest Rate Sensitivity:

   o When interest rates rise, REIT dividends may become less attractive, leading to price drops.

3. Concentration Risk:

   o Some REITs focus heavily on specific property types (e.g., malls or office spaces), which could be impacted by sector-specific downturns.

4. Economic Dependence:

   o Performance depends on economic conditions such as GDP growth, inflation, and employment rates.

How to Invest in REITs in India?

In India, REITs are relatively new but growing rapidly. SEBI (Securities and Exchange Board of India) regulates REITs here.

1. Listed REITs:

   o The most common way to invest is through stock exchanges (e.g., NSE, BSE). Examples include Embassy Office Parks and Mindspace Business Parks.

2. Minimum Investment:

   o The initial investment for Indian REITs has been reduced to as low as ₹10,000-₹15,000, making it accessible to retail investors.

3. Taxation:

    o Dividends are generally taxable as per the investor's income tax slab. Capital gains tax applies if you sell REIT units at a profit.

A Quick Story

Imagine your friend, Ravi. He wanted to invest in real estate but didn't have enough money to buy an office or flat. Then, he learned about REITs. With just ₹15,000, Ravi invested in a REIT focused on office spaces in Bengaluru. Over the year, he received quarterly dividends and watched his money grow, all while sipping chai in his living room. No brokers, no tenants calling at midnight, just stress-free real estate investment!

Should You Invest in REITs?

YES, if:

- You're looking for a regular income source.
- You want exposure to real estate without the hassles of direct ownership.
- You have a medium – to long-term investment horizon.

NO, if:

- You're uncomfortable with market volatility.
- You rely on steady capital appreciation rather than dividend income.

Key Takeaway

REITs are a great way for beginners to step into the world of real estate investments. They're simple, affordable, and professionally managed. Whether you're building wealth for retirement or just diversifying your portfolio, REITs can be a handy tool to grow your money—without the "tenant drama" that comes with owning physical property! 😊

Checklist for Purchasing a Physical Real Estate Property in India

Purchasing real estate is a significant financial decision that requires careful evaluation to avoid potential legal and financial risks. Below is a detailed checklist for purchasing property in India, along with examples and explanations.

1. Determine the Purpose of Purchase

- **Checklist:**

    o Is the property for personal use, investment, or rental income?

    o What is your budget and financial capacity?

    o Are you seeking short-term gains or long-term appreciation?

  Example:

  If buying for personal use, consider factors like location, amenities, and proximity to schools, offices, and hospitals. For investment, assess future development plans and growth potential in the area.

2. Verify Title and Ownership

- **Checklist:**

    o Ensure the seller has a clear and marketable title to the property.

- o Check for any encumbrances or legal disputes.
- o Obtain a certified copy of the sale deed, mutation records, and title search report.

Example:

A title search reveals whether the property is mortgaged or involved in any litigation. A certified legal professional can help verify ownership details.

3. Verify Property Documents

- **Checklist:**
  - o **Sale Deed**: Confirms ownership transfer.
  - o **Mother Deed**: Traces the property's ownership history.
  - o **Encumbrance Certificate**: Confirms no legal or financial liabilities.
  - o **Approval Plan**: Verify the building or layout plan is approved by the local authority.
  - o **Occupancy Certificate (OC)**: Indicates that the property is ready for occupation (mandatory for apartments).
  - o **RERA Registration**: Check if the property is registered under the Real Estate Regulatory Authority (RERA).

Example:

A buyer purchasing an apartment should confirm that the project is RERA-registered to ensure compliance with legal standards.

4. Validate Land Use and Zoning

- **Checklist:**

  o Confirm the property adheres to the master plan and zoning regulations.

  o Check if the property is classified as residential, commercial, or agricultural land.

  o Verify conversion approval for non-residential land.

  Example:

  Purchasing agricultural land for residential development requires legal conversion and approval from local authorities.

5. Check Builder Credentials

- **Checklist:**
- Research the builder's reputation and track record.
- Check past projects and adherence to deadlines.
- Review reviews, ratings, and feedback from previous buyers.

  Example:

  A reputable builder is more likely to deliver on promises and comply with legal and quality standards.

6. Legal Due Diligence

- **Checklist:**

  o Hire a legal expert to examine the property's history, documentation, and litigation status.

- o Verify compliance with local and national laws (e.g., municipal laws, RERA Act).

- o Ensure there are no disputes with co-owners or third parties.

Example:

A legal expert can verify whether a property's boundaries are encroached upon or whether it is part of disputed land.

7. Financial Verification

- **Checklist:**

  - o Compare the property price with prevailing market rates in the area.

  - o Ensure all payments are transparent and accounted for in the sale agreement.

  - o Confirm eligibility for a home loan if financing is required.

Example:

Use property valuation tools or consult real estate agents to determine if the quoted price for a 3-bedroom apartment is justified.

8. Taxation and Registration

- **Checklist:**

  - o Check the applicable **stamp duty** and **registration charges** for the property.

  - o Verify the seller's tax receipts for property tax and other dues.

o Ensure the sale agreement mentions GST (if applicable for under-construction properties).

Example:

In Maharashtra, stamp duty for women buyers is 1% lower than the standard rate. Verify such benefits before payment.

9. Physical Inspection

- **Checklist:**

  o Inspect the property for construction quality, legal boundaries, and area measurements.

  o Cross-check the built-up area with the sale agreement.

  o Ensure there are no structural issues, seepage, or damages.

Example:

A site visit to an under-construction property helps verify progress and adherence to promised timelines.

10. Verify Amenities and Infrastructure

- **Checklist:**

  o Check for promised amenities (e.g., parking, water supply, electricity, lifts, security).

  o Assess infrastructure like roads, public transport, and connectivity.

  o Evaluate proximity to schools, hospitals, and markets.

Example:

A gated community should have functional security systems, playgrounds, and a reliable water supply.

11. Drafting and Signing the Sale Agreement

- **Checklist:**

  o Draft a detailed sale agreement mentioning payment terms, possession date, and penalties for non-compliance.

  o Include a clause for dispute resolution.

  Example:

  A sale agreement should specify that possession will be granted after full payment of INR 1 crore for the villa.

12. Registration and Possession

- **Checklist:**

  o Register the property with the Sub-Registrar's Office.

  o Ensure the property is transferred to your name in all official records (e.g., utility bills, society records).

  o Obtain the keys and completion certificate.

  Example:

  After registration, ensure your name is updated in the municipal records for property tax purposes.

13. Post-Purchase Responsibilities

- **Checklist:**

  o Pay property taxes, maintenance charges, and utility bills on time.

  o Get property insurance for added protection.

Example:

After purchasing a commercial space, ensure you pay annual maintenance charges to the building association.

Conclusion

Purchasing real estate in India involves numerous legal, financial, and technical considerations. Conducting thorough due diligence and seeking professional guidance ensures a smooth and secure transaction. Always retain copies of all documents and maintain a transparent record of all financial transactions.

Risk vs Reward: The Balancing Act

Every investment involves a trade-off between the level of risk and the potential for reward. Understanding this balance is crucial to making informed financial decisions that align with your goals.

Low-Risk Investments: Safety First

Low-risk instruments like Fixed Deposits (FDs), Public Provident Funds (PPFs), and government bonds offer stability and predictable returns. These are suitable for risk-averse investors or for preserving capital during volatile times.

Example: An FD offering 6% annual interest may seem modest, but it ensures your principal is safe. For instance, investing ₹1 lakh in an FD for 5 years at 6% annual interest grows to ₹1.34 lakh. While inflation may slightly erode purchasing power, your funds remain secure.

Pros:

- Predictable returns.
- Minimal volatility.
- Great for short-term goals or emergencies.

Cons:

- Returns may not beat inflation.
- Limited wealth generation potential.

Moderate-Risk Investments: A Balance

Moderate-risk options include balanced mutual funds, NPS, or corporate bonds. These offer a mix of growth and stability by combining equity and debt exposure.

Example: A balanced mutual fund investing 60% in equity and 40% in debt may provide a return of 10% annually. Investing ₹5 lakh could grow to ₹8.05 lakh in 6 years, blending growth potential with reduced risk.

Pros:

- Diversified exposure.
- Better returns than low-risk instruments.

Cons:

- Moderate volatility.
- Not entirely risk-free.

High-Risk Investments: Potential for High Rewards

High-risk instruments such as individual stocks, small-cap mutual funds, or cryptocurrencies can offer substantial returns, but the risks are equally high.

Example: An equity mutual fund focused on small caps may return 15% annually. ₹2 lakh invested for 10 years grows to ₹8.1 lakh. However, these funds are highly sensitive to market conditions, so timing and patience are critical.

Pros:

- High growth potential.
- Opportunities for significant wealth creation.

Cons:

- High volatility.
- Greater likelihood of loss if not carefully managed.

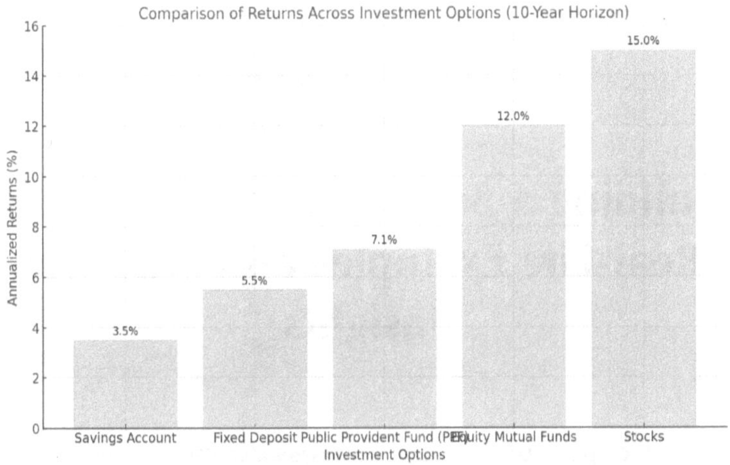

Diversification: Spreading the Risk

"Don't put all your eggs in one basket" is more than just an old saying—it's sound financial advice. Diversification reduces risk by allocating your investments across asset classes, industries, and geographies.

Example of a Diversified Portfolio:

- 50% in equity mutual funds (growth potential).

- 20% in debt instruments (stability).

- 15% in gold or ETFs (hedging).

- 10% in PPF or NPS (retirement security).

- 5% in individual stocks (high-risk, high-reward potential).

Diversification ensures that even if one asset class underperforms, others may compensate, stabilising overall returns.

Key Takeaway: Balance your portfolio based on your risk appetite, financial goals, and investment horizon.

* * * * *

Chapter 8

Building a Balanced Portfolio with Real-Life Examples and Practical Insights

A balanced portfolio is like a Swiss Army knife—prepared to handle any market scenario, whether it's a bull run, a bear market, a pandemic like COVID-19, or global uncertainties like wars. Here's how you can create one, backed by detailed real-world examples and how it serves during challenging times.

Step 1: Define the Balanced Portfolio

A **balanced portfolio** combines growth assets (like equity) with stability assets (like debt, gold, or real estate).

- **Equity:** High growth but volatile.
- **Debt:** Stability and predictable returns.
- **Gold:** Inflation hedge.
- **Real Estate/REITs:** Tangible asset and diversification.

Step 2: Practical Example of a Balanced Portfolio

Let's assume a portfolio worth ₹10 lakhs. Here's how it can be allocated:

Asset Class	Allocation	Investment Examples	Amount (₹)
Equity	50%	Nifty 50 ETF, Infosys, HDFC Bank, TCS	₹5,00,000
Debt	30%	RBI Savings Bonds, ICICI Pru Debt Fund	₹3,00,000
Gold	10%	Sovereign Gold Bonds, Gold ETFs	₹1,00,000
Real Estate/ REITs	10%	Embassy REITs (commercial property exposure)	₹1,00,000

Step 3: How a Balanced Portfolio Performs in Different Scenarios

1. Bull Market (High Growth Period)

In a bull market, equity markets surge, giving massive returns to growth-oriented investments.

Example:

During the **2017 Indian bull market**, the Nifty50 delivered returns of 28.6%.

- Equity allocation (₹5,00,000) grows significantly. If it delivers 25%, your equity value becomes ₹6,25,000.
- Other assets like debt and gold provide modest returns, ensuring stability.

Benefit of a Balanced Portfolio:

Even if one or two stocks underperform, broad exposure through index funds and diversification mitigates risk.

2. Bear Market (Market Crash)

In a bear market, equity markets decline, but other assets like gold and bonds act as cushions.

Example:

During the **2008 financial crisis**, Indian equity markets dropped by 52%, but gold gave a return of 29% that year.

- Equity allocation (₹5,00,000) may fall to ₹2,50,000 (50% loss).

- Gold allocation (₹1,00,000) rises to ₹1,29,000, offsetting some losses.

- Debt instruments remain stable, protecting your portfolio's overall value.

Benefit of a Balanced Portfolio:

Gold and debt stabilise the portfolio during crashes, preventing emotional decisions like panic selling.

3. Pandemic Situation (e.g. COVID-19)

COVID-19 caused a market crash in early 2020, but equity markets recovered dramatically by the end of the year, while gold and debt delivered steady returns.

Example:

- Nifty50 dropped by 38% in March 2020 but delivered 15% annual growth by December.

- Gold prices surged 25% as investors sought safety.
- Debt remained stable, providing liquidity for emergencies.

Portfolio Resilience:

- Equity's recovery ensures long-term gains.
- Gold's surge offsets immediate losses.
- Debt provides liquidity and stability in uncertain times.

4. Global Uncertainty (e.g. Wars or Geopolitical Crises)

Wars or geopolitical tensions lead to market volatility. Commodities like gold rise while equity markets decline.

Example:

During the **Russia-Ukraine war (2022)**:

- Equity markets dropped globally (Nifty50 fell ~15% in March 2022).
- Gold prices rose ~10% in the same period.
- Oil and energy stocks surged, benefiting sectoral funds in energy.

Portfolio Resilience:

- Gold and REITs act as safe havens.
- Diversification across geographies (global funds) protects against localised risks.

Step 4: Why a Balanced Portfolio Works

1. **Reduces Risk:** Combines high-risk equity with low-risk debt and gold.
2. **Stabilises Returns:** During downturns, safe assets (debt, gold) cushion losses.

3. **Captures Growth:** During bull runs, equity generates significant returns.

4. **Hedges Against Inflation:** Gold and real estate protect purchasing power.

5. **Liquidity:** Debt provides cash flow during emergencies.

Step 5: Tips for Managing Your Balanced Portfolio

1. **Rebalance Regularly:** Adjust allocations every 6–12 months to maintain the target ratio.

   For example, if equity grows to 60% of your portfolio after a bull run, sell some and reinvest in gold or debt.

2. **Global Diversification:** Invest in international funds (e.g., S&P 500 ETFs) to reduce dependence on Indian markets.

3. **Emergency Fund:** Keep 6–12 months of expenses in liquid funds or fixed deposits for unforeseen events.

Conclusion

A balanced portfolio ensures you are prepared for all market conditions—bull or bear, pandemics or wars. It's like having an all-terrain vehicle that adapts to smooth highways, rough terrains, or muddy roads. Build your portfolio wisely, rebalance often, and trust the process for steady, long-term wealth creation.

Celebrity Portfolios: Real Examples of Balanced Strategies

Let's analyse real-life portfolios of successful personalities who have demonstrated the principles of diversification, hedging, and balance in their investments. These examples show how these strategies work in action.

1. Warren Buffett (Chairman, Berkshire Hathaway)

Buffett's portfolio is the gold standard for disciplined, long-term investing.

Portfolio Breakdown (2023, Approximate):

- **Equity:** The majority of his investments are in blue-chip companies. Top holdings include:
    - Apple (47% of the portfolio, $150 billion value)
    - Coca-Cola, Bank of America, Chevron.
- **Cash:** 10–15% in cash equivalents (to capitalise on market opportunities).
- **Debt:** Minimal personal investments in bonds, but Berkshire holds significant U.S. Treasury Bills.
- **Real Estate:** Owns modest personal properties but prefers public markets over direct real estate investments.

Lessons for a Balanced Portfolio:

- **Core (Stability):** Investments in stable, dividend-paying stocks like Coca-Cola.
- **Satellite (Growth):** Apple and other growth stocks.
- **Hedging:** Holding cash and Treasuries for liquidity and downturn protection.

2. Rakesh Jhunjhunwala (India's Big Bull)

The late Rakesh Jhunjhunwala was known for his aggressive equity bets but maintained balance through real estate and debt investments.

Portfolio Breakdown (2022):

- **Equity:** Major holdings included Titan, Tata Motors, Star Health, and Metro Brands.

  - Titan: His largest holding, valued at ₹11,000 crore (~40% of the portfolio).

- **Real Estate:** Owned multiple high-value properties in Mumbai, including a ₹400 crore Malabar Hill property.

- **Debt and Fixed Income:** While exact figures are private, he reportedly kept a significant portion in liquid assets like bonds and fixed deposits for stability.

Lessons for a Balanced Portfolio:

- **Core (Stability):** Titan (a well-established company) and real estate investments.

- **Satellite (Growth):** Smaller companies like Star Health for high returns.

- **Hedging:** Diversification across sectors and asset classes.

3. Priyanka Chopra Jonas (Actor and Entrepreneur)

Priyanka has built a global portfolio by combining traditional and alternative investments.

Portfolio Breakdown:

- **Equity:** Investments in startups (e.g., dating app Bumble, tech companies).

- **Real Estate:**

  - Properties in Mumbai, New York, and Los Angeles (~₹150 crore+ combined value).

- **Alternative Investments:**

  o Invested in brands like Perfect Moment (luxury skiwear).

- **Gold and Jewellery:** Likely holds gold in physical and ornamental forms, typical for Indian investors.

Lessons for a Balanced Portfolio:

- **Core (Stability):** Real estate provides steady value growth.

- **Satellite (Growth):** High-risk startup investments.

- **Hedging:** Geographic diversification (India and U.S. assets).

4. Shah Rukh Khan (Actor and Businessman)

SRK has a diversified portfolio focused on luxury real estate and business ventures.

Portfolio Breakdown:

- **Real Estate:**

  o Mannat (Mumbai): ₹200 crore+

  o Properties in Dubai (Palm Jumeirah villa) and London.

- **Business Investments:**

  o Red Chillies Entertainment produces high-grossing films.

  o Ownership stake in Kolkata Knight Riders (IPL).

- **Gold:** Likely holds some gold for traditional purposes.

Lessons for a Balanced Portfolio:

- **Core (Stability):** Real estate assets (global diversification).
- **Satellite (Growth):** High-risk ventures like IPL and film production.
- **Hedging:** Tangible assets like real estate and gold.

Why Celebrity Portfolios Prove Our Point

1. **Diversification Across Asset Classes:**

   o Warren Buffett balances equities with cash reserves.

   o Rakesh Jhunjhunwala diversified into real estate alongside equities.

2. **Hedging Against Risks:**

   o Priyanka Chopra hedges her portfolio with global real estate and alternative assets.

   o Shah Rukh Khan's investment in tangible assets protects against inflation.

3. **Balancing Stability and Growth:**

   o Buffett's Coca-Cola holdings are stable, while Apple drives growth.

   o Rakesh's Titan is stable, while Star Health offers potential high returns.

Conclusion: Why a Balanced Portfolio Always Wins

These real-life portfolios demonstrate that a **balanced strategy** isn't just theory – it's a proven approach to wealth creation. Whether it's during a bull market, a pandemic, or geopolitical crises, diversification and hedging shield investors from extreme losses while capitalising on opportunities.

By applying these lessons, you can create your own portfolio that's not only robust but also tailored to your financial goals and risk appetite. Invest wisely and let your money work for you!

* * * *

Chapter 9

The Power of Compounding: Time as Your Greatest Ally

Albert Einstein called compounding "the eighth wonder of the world". Its magic lies in earning returns on both your initial investment and the returns already generated.

How Compounding Works

Compounding grows your wealth exponentially over time. The longer your investment horizon, the more pronounced the effect.

Formula: Compound Interest Formula

$A = P \times (1 + r/n)^{n*t}$

Where:

- **A** = Final amount (including principal and interest)
- **P** = Principal (initial investment)
- **r** = Annual interest rate (in decimal form, e.g., 5% = 0.05)
- **n** = Number of times interest is compounded per year
- **t** = Time the money is invested for (in years)

Example: Invest ₹1 lakh at 10% annual return:

- After 1 year: ₹1.1 lakh.
- After 10 years: ₹2.59 lakh.

- After 20 years: ₹6.72 lakh. The key is the snowball effect—the returns generated in later years far outweigh those in the beginning.

Story of Two Friends: Rahul and Priya

Rahul starts investing ₹5,000 per month at age 25, while Priya starts the same at 35. Both earn 10% annually and invest until 60.

- **Rahul**: ₹5,000/month for 35 years = ₹1.26 crore.
- **Priya**: ₹5,000/month for 25 years = ₹54.3 lakh.

By starting 10 years earlier, Rahul's corpus is more than double Priya's—even though he only invested ₹6 lakh more.

Lesson: Time is more critical than the amount invested. Start early and let compounding do the heavy lifting.

Real-Life Inspiration: Warren Buffett

Warren Buffett's net worth exceeded $100 billion, largely due to compounding. Starting his investing journey at 11, Buffett allowed decades of consistent growth to multiply his wealth.

Key Tips to Harness Compounding:

1. **Start Early:** Even small amounts grow significantly over time.

2. **Stay Invested:** Avoid frequent withdrawals to let your money grow.

3. **Reinvest Returns:** Keep reinvesting dividends or interest to maximise growth.

4. **Be Patient:** Compounding takes time, so resist the urge to chase short-term gains.

The Cost of Delay

Waiting even a few years to start investing can have a dramatic impact on your wealth.

- Investing ₹5,000/month for 30 years at 12% = ₹1.76 crore.
- Investing the same for 25 years = ₹1.02 crore. A 5-year delay costs ₹74 lakh!

Key Takeaway: Compounding rewards consistency and patience. The earlier you begin, the larger your financial snowball grows.

By understanding the balance of risk and reward and leveraging the power of compounding, you can build a robust investment portfolio. Remember, wealth creation is a marathon, not a sprint. Start now and let time work in your favour.

Rags to Riches: Inspiring Indian Investment Success Stories

1. Rakesh Jhunjhunwala – The Big Bull of the Indian Stock Market

Born into a middle-class family in Mumbai, Rakesh Jhunjhunwala started his stock market journey with just Rs 5,000. Guided by a deep understanding of businesses and an uncanny ability to predict market trends, he turned this modest amount into a portfolio worth billions.

Jhunjhunwala's investments in companies like Titan, Crisil, and Lupin Pharmaceuticals showcased his ability to identify long-term growth stories. Titan, which he bought when the stock was trading at Rs. 3, grew to become one of India's largest consumer brands.

How He Achieved It:

- Patiently holding investments for decades.

- Analysing companies' fundamentals and leadership.

- Staying optimistic during market downturns, leveraging opportunities to buy undervalued stocks.

2. Dolly Khanna – The Homemaker-Turned-Investment Icon

Dolly Khanna, a Chennai-based homemaker, began investing in the stock market in the 1990s with her husband, Rajiv Khanna. They started small but focused on emerging sectors like chemicals, textiles, and sugar. Her portfolio includes stocks like Nilkamal and Rain Industries, which yielded extraordinary returns over time.

Dolly's story proves that with diligence and strategic thinking, even small investors can achieve significant financial success.

How She Achieved It:

- Investing in underappreciated sectors poised for growth.

- Holding onto stocks through volatility to realise their full potential.

- Thorough research and understanding of market cycles.

3. Raamdeo Agrawal – From a Small Town to Billionaire Investor

Raamdeo Agrawal, co-founder of Motilal Oswal Financial Services, came from a small town in Rajasthan. Starting his journey with limited resources, he built immense wealth through disciplined investing. One of his most notable investments was

Hero Honda, which he purchased at Rs. 30 per share and held until it skyrocketed to Rs. 2,600.

Agrawal's belief in the power of compounding and long-term investing made him one of India's most respected investors.

How He Achieved It:

- Adopting the QGLP philosophy (Quality, Growth, Longevity, Price).

- Sticking to businesses with excellent management and scalable models.

- Regularly reviewing his portfolio to align with market opportunities.

4. Ashish Dhawan – Turning Private Equity into Philanthropy

Ashish Dhawan, founder of ChrysCapital, made a fortune through private equity investments. Starting with limited funds, his firm grew by investing in high-growth Indian companies during the early 2000s. One notable success was the investment in Axis Bank, which yielded significant returns.

Dhawan eventually transitioned to philanthropy, focusing on education reform, proving that financial success can fuel societal impact.

How He Achieved It:

- Identifying businesses with high growth potential in emerging markets.
- Diversifying investments across industries.

- Giving back to society, showing the larger purpose of wealth creation.

5. An Individual Investor Success Story: Ravi Gupta

Ravi Gupta, a salaried professional in his 30s, started investing in mutual funds through SIPs (Systematic Investment Plans) with ₹5,000 a month. Over 15 years, his disciplined investing in equity-oriented funds, combined with the power of compounding, turned into a corpus of over ₹1 crore.

Ravi's journey is a testament to how regular investing, even with a modest income, can create wealth over time.

How He Achieved It:

- Staying consistent with monthly SIPs.
- Choosing diversified equity funds with a long-term horizon.
- Avoiding panic selling during market crashes and continuing investments.

Lessons from These Stories

These stories underline the transformative power of investing:

- **Start Small**: Many began with limited resources, proving that consistent investing matters more than starting big.
- **Patience Pays Off**: Wealth creation is a marathon, not a sprint. Long-term commitment amplifies the power of compounding.

- **Research is Key**: Successful investors emphasise understanding market trends, company fundamentals, and economic cycles.

- **Diversify Wisely**: Spreading investments across sectors minimises risks.

- **Keep Emotions in Check**: Market volatility is inevitable. Staying focused on long-term goals ensures success.

Whether you're an aspiring investor or looking to refine your strategy, these stories show that with discipline, knowledge, and patience, anyone can turn investments into significant financial milestones.

Different Platforms for Investing and How to Choose What Suits You Best

Investing is like a buffet – you have plenty of options, but not all dishes suit your taste (or your stomach). Let's explore the platforms available and figure out how you can pick the one that fits you best.

1. Stock Market Platforms

These are apps or websites where you can directly buy and sell stocks, mutual funds, or ETFs. Popular ones in India include **Zerodha**, **Groww**, and **Upstox**.

- **Best for:** Tech-savvy individuals who like hands-on control over investments.

- **Pros**: Transparency, real-time access, and a variety of choices.

- **Cons**: Risky if you don't have time or knowledge.

Pro Tip: If market volatility gives you a mini heart attack, avoid stock-only platforms.

2. Robo-Advisors

Platforms like **ET Money** and **Kuvera** offer automated investment services. They suggest portfolios based on your risk profile and financial goals.

- **Best for**: Beginners who want expert advice without the hefty fees.
- **Pros**: Low cost, goal-oriented, and easy to use.
- **Cons**: Limited customisation for experienced investors.

Pro Tip: Think of this as your investment GPS – great for navigating, but you'll still need to fuel the car.

3. Mutual Fund Platforms

Apps like **Paytm Money, myCAMS,** or directly from AMCs (Asset Management Companies) allow you to invest in mutual funds.

- **Best for**: Those who want professional management without daily involvement.
- **Pros**: Diversified, regulated, and suitable for various goals.
- **Cons**: May have higher fees compared to DIY investing.

Pro Tip: Choose mutual funds if you believe in "let the experts handle it while I relax."

4. Fixed-Income Platforms

Platforms like **Bonds India** or banks themselves offer Fixed Deposits (FDs), bonds, or government schemes like PPF and NSC.

- **Best for**: Risk-averse investors looking for stable returns.
- **Pros**: Safe and predictable.
- **Cons**: Lower returns compared to equities.

Pro Tip: Treat these as your safety cushion, not your primary wealth builder.

5. Real Estate Investment Platforms

New-age platforms like **Realty Shares** or traditional brokers let you invest in real estate or REITs (Real Estate Investment Trusts).

- **Best for**: Investors with long-term goals and higher budgets.
- **Pros**: Tangible assets, potential for rental income.
- **Cons**: High entry costs, lower liquidity.

Pro Tip: If you want a piece of real estate without buying an entire property, REITs are your friend.

6. Digital Gold Platforms

Apps like **PhonePe**, **Google Pay**, and **Paytm** allow you to buy gold in small quantities digitally.

- **Best for**: Gold lovers who don't want to worry about physical storage.
- **Pros**: Convenient, flexible, and easy to liquidate.
- **Cons**: Storage fees for long-term holdings.

Pro Tip: Great for adding shine to your portfolio, but don't overdo it. Gold is more a hedge, not a growth driver.

How to Choose the Right Platform

Here's a quick checklist to find your perfect match:

1. **Know Your Goals**: Are you saving for retirement, a dream car, or just exploring? Different platforms cater to different goals.

   o Do you wish for long-term growth? Stocks and mutual funds.

   o Do you prefer Safety and stability? FDs or bonds.

2. **Understand Your Risk Appetite**:

   o Do you love roller coasters? Go for stocks or crypto.

   o Do you prefer kiddie rides? Choose fixed income or gold.

3. **Assess Your Knowledge and Time**:

   o Do you enjoy analysing companies? Go for direct stocks.

   o Don't have time? Use mutual funds or advisors.

4. **Check Fees and Accessibility**:

   o Apps often charge fees for transactions or account maintenance. Choose one that offers good features within your budget.

5. **Start Small and Experiment**:

   o Don't dive in with your life savings. Test platforms with small amounts and see what feels right.

Final Thought

Investing platforms are like footwear—choose the one that fits your financial journey. It's okay to try on a few before you find the perfect pair. After all, a comfortable platform can make the walk toward wealth much smoother!

* * * * *

Chapter 10

FIRE: Financial Independence, Retire Early

Imagine waking up one fine morning, brewing your favourite cup of chai, and knowing you don't have to log into work unless you choose to. Instead, you can spend your day doing what truly lights you up – whether it's travelling, gardening, painting, or volunteering. This dream, dear reader, is the essence of FIRE: Financial Independence, Retire Early. And it isn't just for the uber-rich; it's for anyone with the right mindset and strategy – yes, even middle-class Indians.

What Is FIRE?

FIRE is a lifestyle movement centred around achieving financial independence early in life so you can retire early – not necessarily to stop working but to have the freedom to work on your terms. It's not about escaping responsibilities but escaping financial stress and societal expectations. Simply put, it's about reclaiming control over your time and life.

The Math Behind FIRE: Your FIRE Number

Your FIRE number is the amount of money you need to invest to cover your annual living expenses without running out of money. The general rule is to multiply your annual expenses by 25. Why 25? Because it's based on the 4% rule – a popular rule in the FIRE community suggesting that you can withdraw 4% of your investments annually without depleting them.

How to Calculate Your FIRE Number

1. **Estimate Your Annual Expenses**: Include everything – housing, food, utilities, healthcare, travel, and leisure. Let's say your annual expense is ₹4,00,000.

2. **Multiply by 25**: ₹4,00,000 x 25 = ₹1 crore.

3. **Adjust for Inflation**: Let's assume an average inflation rate of 6% per year over the next 20 years.

The formula for the future value (FV) of expenses is:

$$FV = \text{Current Expenses} \times (1 + \text{Inflation Rate}) \char`^ \text{Number of Years}$$

For example, if your current annual expense is ₹400,000:

$$FV = ₹400,000 \times (1 + 0.06) \char`^ 20 \approx ₹1,284,000.$$

This means your future annual expense will be approximately ₹12,84,000, and your inflation-adjusted FIRE number will be:

₹12,84,000 x 25 = ₹3.21 crore.

Example: An IT Employee Earning ₹12 LPA

Let's consider an IT professional earning ₹12 lakh per annum (LPA) with annual expenses of ₹6 lakh. Assuming they plan to retire in 20 years, their inflation-adjusted FIRE number can be calculated as follows:

1. **Current Annual Expenses**: ₹6,00,000

2. **Inflation Adjustment (6% per year for 20 years)**: $FV = ₹6,00,000 \times (1 + 0.06) \char`^ 20 \approx ₹19,26,000$

3. **Inflation-Adjusted FIRE Number**: ₹19,26,000 x 25 = ₹4.81 crore.

This means the IT employee needs to accumulate approximately ₹4.81 crore to achieve financial independence while accounting for inflation.

Role Models Who Achieved FIRE

Here are a few inspiring individuals who have walked the FIRE path and achieved financial independence:

1. **Mr. Money Mustache (Pete Adeney):** A former software engineer who retired at 30. Pete shares his journey and insights on his blog, teaching people how to live frugally and invest wisely.

2. **Kristy Shen and Bryce Leung:** This Canadian couple retired in their early 30s after saving aggressively and investing in index funds. Their book *"Quit Like a Millionaire"* breaks down their approach in simple terms.

3. **Ramesh Kumar:** An Indian entrepreneur who achieved FIRE in his early 40s. By investing in mutual funds and cutting down on lavish expenses, he built a corpus large enough to focus on his passion for teaching finance.

4. **Anita Dhawan:** A middle-class homemaker from India who achieved financial independence by leveraging her small tailoring business and systematically investing in gold and mutual funds. Today, she enjoys the freedom to travel and pursue her hobbies.

These role models prove that FIRE is not limited to a specific income bracket or profession. It's about determination, smart planning, and disciplined execution.

Strategies to Achieve FIRE

Achieving FIRE is not about earning millions overnight. It's about small, consistent steps toward financial freedom. Here are some strategies:

1. Aggressive Saving and Smart Investing

- **Save 50% or More of Your Income**: Yes, it sounds ambitious, but it's possible. Cut down on unnecessary expenses, like that gym membership you rarely use or the premium streaming service you barely watch.

- **Invest in High-Growth Assets**: Fixed deposits and savings accounts won't get you to FIRE. Consider mutual funds, index funds, or stocks. A SIP (Systematic Investment Plan) of just ₹20,000 per month, growing at 12% annually, can become ₹1.54 crore in 20 years.

2. Minimalist Living While Enjoying Life

FIRE doesn't mean living like a miser. It means spending intentionally on what brings you joy and cutting out the fluff. Love books? Borrow them from a library or buy them second-hand. Enjoy travelling? Plan budget-friendly trips instead of luxury vacations. Minimalism is about making your life richer with experiences, not stuff.

3. Increasing Your Income Streams

To reach FIRE faster, find ways to increase your income. Consider freelancing, starting a side hustle, or upskilling for a higher-paying job. Think of these as short-term sacrifices for long-term freedom.

Is FIRE Achievable for Middle-Class Indians?

The short answer is yes, with careful planning and discipline. Many middle-class Indians are already halfway there. We're naturally inclined to save, and the joint family system often reduces living costs.

Challenges for Middle-Class Indians:

- **Inflation**: India's inflation can erode savings if you're not investing in assets that outpace it.

- **Healthcare Costs**: Medical expenses can be unpredictable. Adequate health insurance is a must.

- **Family Responsibilities**: Many Indians prioritise children's education and parents' healthcare over their own retirement goals. Balancing these is critical.

Overcoming Barriers to Achieve FIRE

1. **Start Small and Build Momentum**: Begin with saving even 10-20% of your income and gradually increase it as you cut down unnecessary expenses. Every small step counts.

2. **Invest Consistently**: Use SIPs to systematically invest in mutual funds or index funds, which can outpace inflation and grow your wealth over time.

3. **Leverage Your Skills**: Explore side hustles, freelance opportunities, or part-time work to boost your income streams. For example, teaching online or offering consulting services can significantly accelerate your savings.

4. **Reduce Lifestyle Inflation**: As your income grows, resist the urge to spend more. Focus on maintaining a minimalist lifestyle and directing extra earnings toward investments.

5. **Secure Adequate Insurance**: Protect yourself with health and term insurance to mitigate financial shocks from unexpected events.

6. **Set Realistic Goals**: Customise your FIRE number to suit your lifestyle and family needs. Break it into smaller milestones to track your progress and stay motivated.

By addressing these barriers head-on, middle-class Indians can unlock the path to financial independence and enjoy the freedom to live life on their own terms.

FIRE: Freedom to Live Your Best Life

FIRE is not just about money; it's about freedom. Freedom to spend your time doing what you love, to choose work that excites you, to travel, to relax, and to pursue your passions. It's about living intentionally and knowing that life is not a rat race but a journey to savour.

Remember, FIRE isn't a one-size-fits-all formula. Your path will be unique, shaped by your values, goals, and circumstances. Start small, stay consistent, and watch your dreams turn into reality. After all, financial independence isn't just a goal; it's a mindset and a way of life.

So, are you ready to light your FIRE and reclaim your freedom?

* * * * *

PART 04

FINANCIAL FITNESS FOR LIFE

Chapter 11

The Billionaire Blueprint: Habits of Financially Successful People

Success leaves clues. The journey of the world's billionaires isn't a mere stroke of luck—it's the result of habits, discipline, and strategic decision-making. Whether it's Warren Buffett's investment patience or Elon Musk's bold risk-taking, their financial practices hold lessons for us all. Let's decode three key pillars of financial success: long-term vision, leveraging opportunities, and the power of systems.

1. Long-term Vision: The Importance of Patience in Wealth Building

The old adage, *"Rome wasn't built in a day,"* perfectly applies to wealth creation. Most billionaires attribute their success to long-term planning, patience, and consistency.

Statistical Insights

- A study by the National Bureau of Economic Research found that nearly **70% of the world's wealthiest individuals built their fortunes over decades**, primarily through reinvestment and compounding.

- Warren Buffett, one of the world's wealthiest individuals, famously said, *"Someone's sitting in the shade today because someone planted a tree a long time ago."* By the age of 50,

Buffett's net worth was $300 million. By 89, it skyrocketed to $82 billion—a testament to the power of patience and compounding.

Celebrity Example

Jeff Bezos founded Amazon in 1994 as an online bookstore. For nearly a decade, the company reinvested profits instead of pursuing immediate gains. Bezos's foresight enabled Amazon to dominate e-commerce, with his net worth reaching over $150 billion by 2023.

---

2. Leveraging Opportunities: When to Take Calculated Risks

Risk and reward go hand in hand, but successful individuals don't gamble blindly—they take **calculated risks**. This involves analysing the potential upside while preparing for the downside.

Statistical Insights

- According to a 2022 report by CB Insights, **42% of startups fail because they misjudge market demand or take excessive risks.** However, those who succeed often identify niche opportunities and capitalise on them strategically.

- Elon Musk, for example, invested $180 million from his PayPal exit into Tesla, SpaceX, and SolarCity, leaving himself almost broke. His vision and calculated risk-taking paid off, with Tesla becoming a $1 trillion company by 2021.

Celebrity Example

Ratan Tata, the Indian business magnate, exemplifies strategic risk-taking. Despite initial scepticism, he acquired Jaguar Land

Rover for $2.3 billion in 2008 during the financial crisis. Today, the brand contributes significantly to Tata Motors' global profits.

---

3. The Power of Systems: Automating Savings and Investments

Wealthy individuals often emphasise systems over willpower. By automating processes, they eliminate human error, emotional decision-making, and procrastination.

Statistical Insights

- A 2023 Vanguard report revealed that **people who automate savings are 40% more likely to reach their retirement goals** than those who rely on manual contributions.

- Billionaire entrepreneur Mark Cuban advises, *"Put your financial house in order first. Automate your savings, and only then should you think about investments."*

Celebrity Example

Oprah Winfrey, despite her immense earnings, maintains a disciplined financial system. She follows strict budgets, automates her charitable donations, and invests a fixed percentage of her income in diversified assets. Her systematic approach has made her one of the wealthiest and most influential women globally.

Conclusion: Building Your Blueprint

The habits of financially successful people boil down to three principles:

1. **Patience:** Wealth is built over decades, not overnight.

2. **Calculated risks:** Identify opportunities and weigh the odds before jumping in.

3. **Automation:** Let systems do the heavy lifting to maintain discipline.

Adopting these habits doesn't require a billionaire's bank balance—just a shift in mindset. As financial guru Dave Ramsey puts it, *"You don't build wealth with flashy decisions, you build it with smart habits."* So, whether you're saving your first lakh or investing your first crore, these strategies can set you on the path to financial freedom.

Now, the question is: What step will you take today to design your billionaire blueprint?

Detailed Case Study: Dr. Priya's Journey to ₹1 Billion

Let's create a practical roadmap for **Dr. Priya**, a 35-year-old specialist earning ₹24 lakhs annually. Her financial plan accounts for **marriage, kids, vacations, short-term goals**, and **long-term wealth building** while maintaining a balance between living in the present and planning for the future.

Step 1: Current Financial Overview

- **Age:** 35
- **Annual Salary:** ₹24,00,000
- **Take-home After Tax (approx.):** ₹18,00,000
- **Current Savings:** ₹5,00,000
- **Monthly Expenses:** ₹1,00,000 (₹12,00,000 annually)

Savings Available for Investment (Annually): ₹600,000

Step 2: Financial Goals

Short-term (0–5 Years)

1. **Marriage (in 2 Years)**: Estimated Cost ₹10,00,000
2. **First Child's Birth (in 4 years)**: Expenses ₹2,50,000 per year
3. **Vacations**: ₹1,50,000 annually
4. **Emergency Fund**: Build a reserve of ₹9,00,000 (6 months' expenses)

Medium-term (5–15 Years)

1. **Children's Education**: ₹15,00,000–₹20,00,000 per child by age 18
2. **Home Purchase**: Budget ₹1.5 crore in 10 years
3. **Upgrading Skills for Higher Income**: ₹5,00,000 (specialised certifications)

Long-term (15–35 Years)

1. **Retirement Corpus**: ₹10 crores
2. **Billionaire Goal**: ₹100 crores through investments, real estate, and business ventures.

Step 3: Budgeting for Life Events

Years 1–5: Marriage and First Child

- Dr. Priya sets aside the following:

  - ₹**1,000,000** for marriage over two years.
  - ₹**300,000 annually** into an emergency fund.

- The remaining ₹3,00,000 is invested in equity mutual funds.

Investment Strategy:

- **60% in Mutual Funds (Equity & Hybrid):** ₹1,80,000/year
- **20% in Fixed Deposits/NPS:** ₹60,000/year
- **20% in Gold ETFs:** ₹60,000/year

Projected Returns After 5 Years:

- Investments grow at an average of **10% annual return**, compounding to ₹20,00,000.

Year 6–15: Home Purchase, Kids' Education

1. Dr. Priya and her spouse upgrade their income by:

   o Dr. Priya specialises further, increasing her salary to ₹40,00,000 per year.

   o Spouse contributes ₹1,500,000 per year.

2. They pool their savings and take a **home loan of ₹1 crore** for a property worth ₹1.5 crore. EMI: ₹1 lakh/month.

3. They start an education fund for their child, investing ₹5,00,000/year in index funds.

Budget Allocation During Years 6–15:

- **EMI on Home Loan:** ₹12,00,000 annually
- **Education Fund:** ₹5,00,000 annually
- **Vacation Fund:** ₹2,00,000 annually

- **Emergency Fund Maintenance**: ₹1,00,000 annually
- **Wealth Investments (Equity/Real Estate)**: ₹10,00,000 annually

Step 4: Leveraging Real Estate and Business Ventures (Age 45–55)

By her mid-40s:

1. Dr. Priya starts a **diagnostic centre** with ₹50,00,000 in initial investment (from accumulated wealth and loans).

2. The centre generates an annual profit of ₹25,00,000, reinvested into expanding services.

3. Simultaneously, she invests in rental properties, creating **₹10,00,000/year passive income.**

Step 5: Long-term Wealth Building (Age 55–70)

Portfolio Projection by Age 70:

1. **Equity Mutual Funds and Index Funds:** ₹30 crores (consistent investments + compounding)

2. **Real Estate Holdings:** ₹20 crores (property value + rental income reinvestments)

3. **Diagnostic Centre and Other Ventures:** ₹50 crores

Balancing Lifestyle and Wealth

1. **Vacations:** Dr. Priya ensures annual family trips, spending ₹2,00,000–₹3,00,000 yearly.

2. **Lifestyle Upgrades**: Maintains a balance between lifestyle inflation (max 5% annually) and disciplined savings.

3. **Kids' Education Abroad**: Invests in dollar-linked funds for predictable costs.

Final Takeaway: The Power of Consistency and Planning

Dr. Priya's success lies in **early investments, disciplined saving, and strategic risk-taking**. Despite life's milestones, she stays consistent:

- *10% of income is always invested in high-growth assets.*

- *Business and real estate provide passive income to supplement savings.*

By combining compounding, diversification and discipline, she not only secures her family's future but also achieves her dream of becoming a billionaire by age 70.

Evidence-Based Money Management: A Guide to Smarter Financial Decisions

Managing money is like managing health: it's all about discipline, awareness, and making the right decisions based on facts, not feelings. Unfortunately, many people fall into emotional traps or cognitive biases when it comes to their finances. Let's dive into evidence-based money management with logical decision-making, evidence-backed strategies, and the importance of reviewing and adjusting through an annual financial check-up.

Logical Decision-Making: Avoiding Cognitive Biases and Emotional Traps

The Trap: Emotional Spending

Ever bought something because it *felt* good at the moment but regretted it later? You're not alone. **Emotional spending** is a universal problem exacerbated by targeted advertising. According to a 2023 survey, **57% of Indians admitted to making impulsive purchases online during sales.**

Short Story:

Ramesh, a 30-year-old doctor, always bought the latest gadgets. The dopamine rush of holding a shiny new phone gave him temporary joy, but it didn't last. When he reviewed his finances one day, he was shocked to find that his tech purchases accounted for 30% of his income over the past two years. That money could have grown significantly if invested.

How to Avoid This Trap

1. **Pause Before You Purchase:** Wait 24 hours before buying anything above ₹5,000.

2. **Track Expenses:** Apps like YNAB (You Need a Budget) or a simple Excel sheet can help you see where your money goes.

3. **Set Goals:** When you know your savings are tied to a future goal (like a house down payment or a vacation), you're less likely to spend impulsively.

Learning from Data: Evidence-Backed Investment Strategies

Why Guess When You Have Data?

Data-driven investment decisions outperform gut-based ones. The **S&P BSE Sensex** delivered an average annual return of **11.2%** over the past **30 years**, yet many retail investors pulled out during temporary market dips, fearing further losses. Data shows that staying invested during market fluctuations leads to better long-term outcomes.

Short Story:

Priya, a school teacher, was terrified when the market dropped in 2020 during the pandemic. She wanted to sell her mutual fund investments. Her financial advisor showed her a graph of market recoveries after crashes. Trusting the data, she stayed invested. By 2022, her portfolio grew by 35%, proving the wisdom of patience.

Evidence-Backed Strategies for Beginners

1. **Diversification is Key:** Don't put all your eggs in one basket. According to a **2022 Morningstar report,** diversified portfolios were 28% less volatile than concentrated ones.

2. **Start Early:** A person investing ₹5,000 monthly from age 25 can accumulate over **₹1 crore** by 60, assuming a 12% annual return. Starting at 35 reduces this to just **₹38 lakh.**

3. **Index Funds Work:** Warren Buffett famously bet on the S&P 500 index fund beating hedge funds—and won. Index funds in India, like the Nifty 50, are cost-effective and deliver consistent returns.

Reviewing and Adjusting: The Annual Financial Check-Up

Why It's Non-Negotiable

Think of your finances like your health. Just as you get an annual medical check-up, you need a financial check-up to ensure your money is working for you. Yet, only **25% of Indians** regularly review their finances, according to a 2022 survey by ET Wealth.

What to Check:

1. **Budget vs. Reality:** Did you overspend or undersave? Why?

2. **Investment Portfolio:** Rebalance if one asset class (like equities) is dominating.

3. **Emergency Fund:** Is it enough for 6-12 months of expenses?

4. **Insurance Coverage:** Are your health and life insurance policies adequate?

Short Story:

Rahul and Meera, a young couple, didn't review their life insurance coverage after the birth of their first child. A financial planner pointed out that their existing plan would fall short in case of an emergency. They upgraded their policy, ensuring peace of mind.

Reviewing Through Metrics

- **Net Worth Calculation:** Has it grown? Use the formula:
- **Net Worth = Total Assets – Total Liabilities.**
- **Debt-to-Income Ratio:** Keep it under 40%.
- **Savings Rate:** Aim to save at least 20% of your income.

Approach to Money

Money isn't just about numbers; it's about life. Every rupee you save and invest today has the potential to build a future filled with opportunities and security. Logical decisions, supported by evidence, allow you to bypass short-term emotions and focus on long-term gains.

Think of your financial journey like this: You're planting a tree. Emotional spending is like chopping it down for firewood. Evidence-based money management is like watering and nurturing the tree, allowing it to grow and provide shade for years to come.

Remember, managing your money isn't about deprivation. It's about living smarter and dreaming bigger. Start today, and your future self will thank you.

Common Pitfalls in Investing

1. Day Trading: The Shortcut That Cuts Deep

The Mistake:

Day trading is alluring because it promises quick money. However, the reality is harsh. According to a **SEBI report (2022), 90% of day traders lose money** in their first year.

Short Story:

Ravi, a software engineer, got hooked on day trading during the pandemic. With no prior experience, he bought and sold stocks within hours, believing he could beat the market. In six months, he lost ₹2 lakh. Ravi realised that even professional traders struggle, and the market doesn't reward overconfidence.

The Lesson:

Invest, don't gamble. SEBI warns retail investors about the risks of speculative trading and encourages long-term investments in diversified portfolios.

2. Futures and Options: A Double-Edged Sword

The Mistake:

Futures and options (F&O) seem sophisticated but are inherently risky. **SEBI's 2023 study revealed that 87% of retail investors in F&O experienced net losses.** Many fail to understand the complexity and leverage involved, leading to financial disaster.

Short Story:

Sandeep, a first-time investor, entered the options market after hearing about high returns from his friends. A single bad trade wiped out half of his savings, leaving him with sleepless nights and mounting regret.

The Lesson:

SEBI has cautioned that derivatives are not suitable for beginners. Stick to simpler investments like mutual funds or index funds unless you thoroughly understand F&O risks.

3. Hearsay Investing: Following the Herd

The Mistake:

Investing based on tips from friends, family, or WhatsApp groups often leads to poor outcomes. What worked for someone else may not work for you.

Short Story:

Sunita heard from her neighbour that a pharmaceutical stock was about to "explode." She invested ₹50,000 without research. The company later faced regulatory issues, and its stock price plummeted. She learned the hard way that hearsay investing is like driving blindfolded.

The Lesson:

Research before investing. SEBI advises investors to verify claims through official company disclosures and reports available on their website.

4. News-Driven Decisions: Reacting Instead of Acting

The Mistake:

Buying or selling stocks based on headlines leads to emotional and hasty decisions. Markets often price in the news before retail investors can act.

Short Story:

During a budget announcement, Ajay sold his banking stocks in a panic, fearing policy changes. The very next day, the market rebounded, and the banking sector rallied. His losses could have been avoided with patience.

The Lesson:

Stay calm during market volatility. SEBI suggests focusing on long-term fundamentals rather than short-term news cycles.

5. Overpriced Buying: Chasing Hot Stocks

The Mistake:

Retail investors often chase stocks at their peak, fearing they'll miss out on profits. This "Fear of Missing Out" (FOMO) leads to overpaying for stocks.

Short Story:

Meena bought shares of a popular tech company at ₹3,000 each during a bull run, believing it was unstoppable. A market correction soon followed, and the stock fell to ₹1,800, eroding her investment value.

The Lesson:

Don't buy stocks just because they're trending. Analyse valuations using metrics like the **price-to-earnings (P/E) ratio** or consult a financial advisor.

6. Buying Penny Stocks: Searching for Multibaggers

The Mistake:

Many retail investors believe cheap penny stocks will deliver multibagger returns. However, most such stocks are fundamentally weak.

Short Story:

Arjun invested in a ₹2 penny stock, hoping it would skyrocket. Instead, the company declared bankruptcy, and the stock became worthless. He later discovered that penny stocks are often manipulated by operators.

The Lesson:

SEBI frequently warns investors about pump-and-dump schemes involving penny stocks. Avoid them unless you're ready to lose your entire investment.

Key SEBI Guidelines for Investors

- **Verify Company Information:** Use SEBI's website and stock exchange disclosures to validate claims.

- **Avoid Speculation:** SEBI advises against speculative trading like F&O and penny stocks for inexperienced investors.

- **Be Cautious of Tips:** SEBI warns against acting on unverified advice or rumours from unofficial sources.

- **Long-Term Focus:** SEBI advocates investing for the long term in well-researched securities or mutual funds.

Conclusion: A Smarter Path Forward

Investment mistakes are costly but avoidable. Evidence-based strategies and adherence to SEBI guidelines can protect you from falling into these traps. Think of investing like planting a tree—patience, care, and proper nurturing will yield fruit. Avoid shortcuts, stay informed, and let your investments grow steadily over time.

Final Thought:

A disciplined approach is like a lighthouse guiding your financial ship through turbulent waters. Stay the course, and you'll reach your destination safely.

* * * *

Chapter 12

The Value of Education and Financial Literacy: Protecting Your Hard-Earned Money

Imagine planting a sapling. You water it daily, protect it from harsh weather, and ensure it grows into a strong tree. Your money is no different. It's your hard-earned sapling, nurtured through sweat, sacrifice, and countless hours of work. Neglect it or hand it to the wrong person, and you risk losing it all.

This is where **education and financial literacy** play a crucial role. Let's understand why they matter and how to avoid the traps of influencers and brokers.

Why Education and Financial Literacy Matter

1. Empowerment to Make Smart Decisions

Financial literacy gives you the tools to understand where to invest, how to save, and how to avoid scams. Without it, you're like a traveller with no map.

Fact: A 2022 SEBI survey revealed that **76% of Indian adults lacked basic financial knowledge.** Many relied on hearsay or unverified sources, leading to poor decisions.

2. Avoiding Costly Mistakes

Understanding terms like **compound interest, asset allocation,** and **diversification** can prevent you from falling for high-risk schemes or overpaying for products you don't need.

Short Story:

Pooja, a young doctor, was sold a complicated ULIP (Unit Linked Insurance Plan) by her bank's agent. She thought it was an investment, but most of her premium went towards insurance charges. Years later, she realised she could have earned double with a simple mutual fund.

The Trap of Influencers and Brokers

1. Influencers: Style Over Substance

Many financial influencers offer advice without being qualified. Their flashy videos and promises of quick wealth might sound appealing, but they often lack depth or research.

Example:

A popular Instagram influencer recently promoted a "guaranteed returns" stock-picking app. SEBI flagged the app as a scam, yet thousands of followers had already invested.

How to Avoid:

- Check the qualifications of influencers. Do they have certifications like **CFA, CFP, or SEBI-registered Investment Advisor?**

- Never act solely on free advice. Research independently or consult a licensed expert.

2. Brokers: Selling, Not Helping

Brokers often push products that earn them higher commissions, not what's best for you. Many retail investors fall into this trap, buying complex insurance products or unnecessary add-ons.

Short Story:

Raj, a retired teacher, invested his life savings in high-commission debentures suggested by his broker. When the company defaulted, he lost everything. He later realised the broker earned hefty fees while he bore the risk.

How to Avoid:

- Understand the product before investing. Ask: *How does this work? What are the risks?*

- Use platforms like **direct mutual funds** to bypass middlemen and save on commissions.

It's Your Hard-Earned Money, Treat It Like Your Kid

Think of your money as your child. Would you hand your child to a stranger without checking their background? No! You'd ensure they're in safe, nurturing hands. Similarly:

- **Learn before you leap:** Educate yourself about financial products before investing.

- **Be cautious:** Avoid impulsive decisions based on flashy ads or peer pressure.

- **Trust but verify:** Even when consulting professionals, cross-check their advice.

How to Start Your Financial Literacy Journey

1. **Books to Read:**

    o *The Psychology of Money* by Morgan Housel

    o *Rich Dad Poor Dad* by Robert Kiyosaki

    o *Let's Talk Money* by Monika Halan

2. **Free Online Resources:**

    o SEBI Investor Education Portal

    o RBI Financial Awareness campaigns

3. **Courses to Consider:**

4. Platforms like Coursera, Khan Academy, and Zerodha Varsity offer free or affordable financial literacy courses.

Conclusion: The Most Important Investment Is in Yourself

Financial literacy is not an expense – it's an investment. It protects your hard-earned money from mistakes, scams, and wrong advice. Remember, no influencer or broker will care for your wealth as much as you do. Treat your money with love and vigilance, like you would a child, and it will grow to secure your future.

Your money is your responsibility. Guard it. Nurture it. Let it thrive.

* * * * *

Chapter 13

Sustainable Financial Practices: Ethical Investing and Minimalism

1. Ethical Investing

Ethical investing, often referred to as ESG (Environmental, Social, and Governance) investing, focuses on aligning financial goals with personal values. By investing in companies that prioritise sustainability, social responsibility, and ethical governance, investors can contribute to a better world while achieving financial returns.

Why It Matters:

- Ethical companies often outperform peers over the long term due to better risk management and customer loyalty.

- Investors can support industries like renewable energy, green technology, and socially impactful ventures.

How to Start:

- Look for ESG mutual funds or ETFs that invest in companies with high sustainability scores.

- Research companies' environmental and social initiatives before investing.

- Avoid sectors like tobacco, fossil fuels, or arms manufacturing if they conflict with your values.

Real-Life Example

2. Minimalism in Financial Life

Minimalism is not just about decluttering your home; it's about simplifying your financial life to focus on what truly matters. By reducing unnecessary expenses and avoiding consumerism, minimalism can lead to greater savings and financial freedom.

Why It Matters:

- Helps eliminate financial stress by reducing debt and unnecessary commitments.

- Encourages intentional spending, ensuring money is used for meaningful purposes.

How to Practice Minimalism:

- **Declutter Financial Products**: Avoid holding multiple credit cards or unnecessary insurance policies.

- **Adopt the 24-Hour Rule**: Delay impulse purchases by waiting 24 hours to evaluate if it's truly needed.

- **Focus on Experiences**: Spend on experiences like travel or learning rather than accumulating material possessions.

- **Create a Capsule Budget**: Allocate funds only to essential categories and a few discretionary ones.

Real-Life Example: A young couple in Bengaluru adopted minimalism by selling their second car, cancelling unused subscriptions, and downsizing their home. This allowed them to save aggressively and invest in their children's education and retirement.

Lessons from Global Trends

- **Sustainable Practices are Profitable**: Companies and individuals adopting ethical and minimalist practices are often more resilient in economic downturns.

- **Long-Term Impact**: Ethical investing ensures your wealth contributes to building a sustainable future.

- **Simplicity Equals Clarity**: Minimalism helps declutter financial decisions, reducing stress and enabling better investment choices.

Incorporating these practices into your financial life isn't just about growing wealth – it's about doing so responsibly and intentionally, creating a lasting positive impact for you and the world.

* * * * *

Chapter 14

The True Purpose of Money: A Zen Perspective

Ah, money—like a flowing river, it has the power to nurture life or to sweep one away in its current. Acknowledge its presence, for it is but a tool, not a tyrant. Use it wisely, and it will support your family and community, uplift your passions, and allow you to walk the path of your values. But surrender to it, and it becomes a master, chaining you to an endless chase.

Money as a Tool

Think of money as a seed. When planted in fertile soil—your dreams, values, and aspirations—it grows into a tree that provides shade and sustenance not just for you but for all those around you. Use its fruits to care for your loved ones, to nurture your community, and to spread kindness.

Pursue Your Passions

Imagine the joy of a painter with a blank canvas or a singer with a melody. Money can buy the canvas, the colours, or the time to sing, but it cannot create the art itself. Let it pave the road for your passions, but do not mistake it for the road itself.

Live Aligned with Your Values

What is wealth if it takes you away from your truth? A bag of gold in a house without peace is heavy to carry. Let money be a bridge to a life that reflects your inner self – a life of honesty, kindness, and purpose.

Defining "Enough": The Art of Balance

Pause and reflect: *What is enough for me?* Chasing more and more is like drinking saltwater; the thirst never ends. Know your enough—not too little to shrink your spirit, nor too much to drown your joy. *"The right balance is when your wealth supports your well-being without overwhelming or limiting you."*

Financial Freedom and a Meaningful Life

True freedom is not in accumulating money but in mastering it. When your needs are met and your heart is light, you are free to create, to give, and to love. Money becomes a silent partner in the orchestra of your life, playing its part without overshadowing the melody.

Money is energy; let it flow to you and through you. Allow it to grow and nourish, but never let it hold you captive. Be its master, not its servant. When you walk this path, money will no longer be a burden or a battle—it will simply be a tool, helping you craft a life of meaning and joy.

Money, when used wisely, can be a force for immense good, transforming not just individual lives but entire communities and the world. Here are some inspiring examples of how people and organisations have converted wealth into human well-being:

1. Eradicating Diseases

The Bill & Melinda Gates Foundation

With billions in funding, the Gates Foundation has focused on eradicating diseases like malaria and polio. By investing in vaccines, healthcare infrastructure, and education, it has saved millions of lives and improved global health, especially in underserved areas.

Lesson: Money can heal the world by empowering science and medicine.

2. Educating the Future

Azim Premji Foundation

In India, Azim Premji, the founder of Wipro, pledged most of his wealth to improve public education. His foundation supports teacher training, builds schools, and promotes equitable access to quality education for children in rural areas.

Lesson: Wealth can be the foundation of a brighter, educated future.

3. Providing Clean Water

Charity: Water

This non-profit uses donations to bring clean drinking water to communities in developing nations. Every dollar translates directly into wells, filtration systems, and sustainable water solutions, changing lives by eliminating waterborne diseases and saving women and children the hours they'd otherwise spend fetching water.

Lesson: A small act of giving can ripple out into large-scale transformation.

4. Empowering Women

Self-Help Groups in India

Through microfinance initiatives, women in rural India have been given small loans to start businesses. This has empowered them financially, improved household incomes, and boosted community development. Grameen Bank in Bangladesh is another success story, proving that small investments can make a big impact.

Lesson: Money can break the cycle of poverty by empowering individuals.

5. Supporting Environmental Sustainability

Patagonia's "Earth Tax"

Outdoor gear company Patagonia donates 1% of its sales to environmental causes. This commitment has helped fund reforestation, ocean cleanups, and climate change research, showing that businesses can use wealth to sustain the planet.

Lesson: Profit can coexist with purpose, benefiting both humanity and nature.

6. Feeding the Hungry

Akshaya Patra Foundation

In India, Akshaya Patra runs the world's largest mid-day meal programme, ensuring millions of children in schools get nutritious meals. This initiative not only fights hunger but also encourages school attendance.

Lesson: Money can nourish bodies and minds, creating a healthier society.

7. Housing for All

Habitat for Humanity

This organisation uses donations to build affordable housing for families in need across the globe. Volunteers work alongside beneficiaries, creating homes and hope.

Lesson: Wealth can build not just walls, but futures.

8. Disaster Relief and Rehabilitation

The Tata Group's Philanthropy

After natural disasters like the Indian Ocean tsunami, the Tata Group has funded large-scale rehabilitation projects, including building homes, hospitals, and schools. Its focus on sustainable recovery ensures long-term benefits for affected communities.

Lesson: Money can rebuild shattered lives with dignity and care.

9. Arts and Culture for Society

Carnegie Libraries

Andrew Carnegie, an industrialist, used his wealth to build over 2,500 libraries worldwide, believing knowledge was the key to uplifting humanity. His philanthropy made education and culture accessible to millions.

Lesson: Money can preserve and share humanity's collective wisdom.

10. Promoting Mental Health

Mental Health Foundations

Organisations like the Live Love Laugh Foundation (founded by Deepika Padukone) use donations to raise awareness, destigmatise mental health issues, and provide support for those struggling with depression and anxiety.

Lesson: Wealth can bring light to hidden battles, creating a more compassionate world.

Final Thought

Money is a tool – a neutral force that reflects the intentions of the person holding it. When directed toward collective well-being, it becomes a powerful catalyst for positive change. Whether through large donations or small acts of kindness, wealth can transform the world into a more just, equitable, and compassionate place.

The Doctor's Prescription for Financial Health: Key Takeaways

1. **Know Your Financial Vital Signs**

   Just like BP and sugar levels tell us about physical health, your income, expenses, savings, and investments reveal your financial health. Track them regularly.

2. **First, Do No Harm (to Your Finances)**

   Avoid unnecessary debts, impulsive spending, and risky investments. Prevention is better than cure, even in financial matters!

3. **Emergency Fund = Financial First Aid Kit**

   Build an emergency fund with 6 months' expenses. It's your safety net for life's unexpected twists.

4. **Invest for Growth, Not Just Safety**

   Savings are like plain rice; investments are nutrition! Learn about mutual funds, stocks, and SIPs for long-term wealth creation.

5. **Cure Debt, Don't Ignore It**

High-interest debts are like chronic diseases—treat them immediately! Tackle the highest-interest debts first with discipline.

6. **Insurance is Your Financial Vaccine**

Get adequate health and life insurance. Don't confuse it with investment – insurance protects, and investments grow.

7. **Plan for Retirement Early**

Retirement is not the end; it's the golden phase. Start investing in PPF, NPS, or mutual funds as early as possible.

8. **Budget Like a Pro**

9. **Follow the 50-30-20 rule:**

   o   50% for needs

   o   30% for wants

   o   20% for savings/investments

Budgeting keeps your financial health in check.

10. **Avoid Financial Quacks**

Be wary of "get-rich-quick" schemes and poorly researched advice. Consult trusted financial planners or learn yourself.

11. **Tax Planning is a Preventive Check-Up**

Don't rush during March. Understand deductions like 80C, 80D, and tax-saving investments.

12. **Health is Wealth—Literally**

    Medical emergencies can drain your finances. Stay healthy to save on healthcare costs and prioritise health insurance.

13. **Start Small, Stay Consistent**

    Small savings and disciplined investments grow over time. Consistency is the secret to wealth.

14. **Write Your Financial Prescription**

    Set goals – short-term, medium-term, and long-term. A clear plan helps you prioritise and stay motivated.

15. **Money Can Amplify Life, Not Buy Happiness**

    Don't let money control your life. Spend wisely on what truly matters: experiences, loved ones, and peace of mind.

Final Thoughts

This journey has been such a mix of dreams, challenges, and little joys. It's not just about plans or projects; it's about finding meaning in everything I do—whether it's writing a book, planning a trip, or simply figuring out how to live better every day.

There's been a constant effort to simplify life—not to make it less, but to make it clear. To focus on what truly matters: health, purpose, relationships, and happiness. Along the way, I've realised that even small steps, like a morning walk or choosing a journal that actually works, can feel like big wins.

I've loved chasing big dreams too—writing a book to help others with their finances, dreaming of a world tour, or even starting a blog that talks about life's big questions. It's exciting and a little scary, but it's also what keeps me going.

Through all of this, I've learned that it's okay to not have everything figured out. What matters is showing up every day, trying, failing, laughing, and trying again. Life isn't perfect, and it doesn't need to be. It's about progress, not perfection.

This is just the beginning. There's so much more to explore, create, and share. And honestly, I can't wait to see where the next steps take me.

* * * *

Glossary of Financial Terms

A

- **Asset Allocation:** The process of dividing your investments among different asset classes, such as equity, debt, and gold, to balance risk and reward.

- **Assets:** Resources owned by an individual or business that have economic value, such as property, stocks, or cash.

B

- **Balanced Portfolio:** An investment strategy that combines various asset classes to reduce risk while achieving growth.

- **Budget:** A financial plan that outlines income, expenses, and savings over a specific period.

C

- **Compound Interest:** Interest calculated on the initial principal and the accumulated interest from previous periods.

- **Credit Score:** A numerical representation of a person's creditworthiness based on their borrowing and repayment history.

D

- **Debt-to-Income Ratio:** A measure of an individual's monthly debt payments compared to their gross monthly income.

- **Diversification**: Spreading investments across various financial instruments or sectors to reduce risk.

E

- **Emergency Fund**: A savings reserve to cover unexpected financial needs, such as medical emergencies or job loss.
- **Equity**: Ownership in a company, typically represented by stocks.

F

- **Fixed Deposit (FD)**: A financial instrument where money is locked in for a fixed term at a predetermined interest rate.
- **FIRE (Financial Independence, Retire Early)**: A lifestyle movement focused on saving and investing aggressively to achieve financial freedom early in life.

G

- **Gold ETFs (Exchange-Traded Funds)**: Investment funds that track the price of gold and trade on stock exchanges like shares.
- **Gross Income**: Total earnings before deductions like taxes and retirement contributions.

H

- **Health Insurance**: A financial product that covers medical expenses.
- **HRA (House Rent Allowance)**: A salary component for employees to cover rental housing costs.

I

- **Index Funds**: Mutual funds or ETFs designed to replicate the performance of a specific market index, like the Nifty 50.
- **Inflation**: The rate at which the general level of prices for goods and services rises over time, reducing purchasing power.

L

- **Liquidity**: The ease with which an asset can be converted into cash without affecting its market price.
- **Loan-to-Value Ratio (LTV)**: The ratio of a loan amount to the appraised value of an asset, typically used in mortgages.

M

- **Mutual Fund**: A financial vehicle pooling money from multiple investors to invest in securities like stocks, bonds, and other assets.
- **Market Capitalisation**: The total value of a company's shares outstanding,

  Calculated as the share price multiplied by the total number of shares.

N

- **Net Worth**: The total value of an individual's assets minus their liabilities.
- **NPS (National Pension System)**: A government-backed retirement savings scheme in India.

P

- **PPF (Public Provident Fund)**: A long-term savings scheme in India with tax benefits and guaranteed returns.
- **Portfolio**: A collection of financial investments, including stocks, bonds, and real estate.

R

- **Recurring Deposit (RD)**: A savings scheme where a fixed amount is deposited regularly for a predetermined period.
- **REITs (Real Estate Investment Trusts)**: Companies that own and manage income-generating real estate assets.

S

- **SIP (Systematic Investment Plan)**: A method of investing a fixed amount in mutual funds at regular intervals.
- **Stock**: A share representing partial ownership in a company.

T

- **Tax Deduction**: An expense that can be subtracted from gross income to reduce taxable income.
- **Term Insurance**: A life insurance policy providing coverage for a specific period.

W

- **Wealth Creation**: The process of accumulating assets over time through investments and savings.

Y

- **Yield**: The income generated from an investment, usually expressed as a percentage of the investment's cost.